# Angering in the Family

# ABOUT THE TITLE—
# "ANGERING IN THE FAMILY"

Choice Theory defines all behavior as being total behavior and states that it is designated by verbs, usually infinitives and gerunds, and named by the component that is most recognizable. Therefore, *angering* is the chosen total behavior of acting out in anger. Within the family this takes many forms from low levels of intensity to rage and aggressive violence against and between family members—father and mother, parent and child, or between siblings. This book discusses the various forms of angering that are found within the family and alternate ways to cope with and reduce the frustrations that are a result of differences between the world as we perceive it and the world as we would like it.

# Angering in the Family

Using Choice Theory to Stop Controlling with Anger

*J. Thomas Bellows, Ph.D.*

iUniverse, Inc.

New York  Lincoln  Shanghai

Angering in the Family
Using Choice Theory to Stop Controlling with Anger

Copyright © 2005 by J. Thomas Bellows, Ph.D.

iUniverse books may be ordered through booksellers or by contacting:

iUniverse
2021 Pine Lake Road, Suite 100
Lincoln, NE 68512
www.iuniverse.com
1-800-Authors (1-800-288-4677)

Cover adapted from a photograph taken by J. Thomas Bellows, Ph.D. of the Angry Boy statue in Vigeland Sculpture Park, Oslo, Norway.

ISBN-13: 978-0-595-35509-9 (pbk)
ISBN-13: 978-0-595-79997-8 (ebk)
ISBN-10: 0-595-35509-9 (pbk)
ISBN-10: 0-595-79997-3 (ebk)

Printed in the United States of America

I also wish to dedicate this book to my wife, Jill and my sons John and Colin. They provided much information for me to use in my self-evaluation and the acceptance of Choice Theory as my intended way of life. They gave me support and assistance while I was writing this book. Without their caring behavior, this book never would have come into being.

# Contents

# ACKNOWLEDGEMENTS

I wish to thank William Glasser, M.D., Carleen Glasser, M.A., Brandi Roth, Ph.D. and the other faculty of the William Glasser Institute and the Choice Theory community. They gave of their valuable time to help me learn reality therapy and Choice Theory and their participation in role-playing that gave me experience in using what I learned with my domestic violence clients. A special appreciation goes to Rita Janos, M.A., and William Glasser, M.D. who reviewed the drafts and made many helpful suggestions. Thanks to all of you.

# FOREWORD

This is a very much needed book. Millions of lives are being made miserable, many wives and some children are being killed daily by angry husbands and fathers. In this book, Dr. Bellows explains how he uses the **Choice Theory** I have created to teach angry husbands and fathers how to control their anger and get along better with their wives and families.

As you will find out from reading this book, choice theory is an effective theory that can help any unhappy relationship. As shown in the book, angry men can be taught **Choice Theory** in groups, which is highly cost effective, and, even more, group members find it to be valuable and even enjoyable to learn. Literally, they have grown up without learning the most important knowledge we all need to know: how to get along well with the important people in their lives. For angry men who can read this book alone may be able to start them in the direction they need to go.

William Glasser, M.D.
Founder of reality therapy
and President of the
William Glasser Institute

# ENDORCEMENTS

"Dr. J. Thomas Bellows openly addresses that which many shy away from or choose not to talk about. He is a champion in his field as he guides those in need (and those not addressing the fact that they have a need) to take the steps to choose positive behaviors. Dr. Bellows firsthand stories and professional experience bring anger and relationships to light as well as the many difficult behaviors affecting daily life. Readers will make personal discoveries as they read *Angering in the Family* and will find that sometimes it is the little things coming to the surface that bring relevant choices and change. Dr. Bellows' reader friendly book is a true masterpiece to help readers master a difference in their lives and those around them."

—**Gail Small**
Fulbright Memorial Scholar
People to People Ambassador
Author: *Joyful Learning: No One Ever Wants To Go To Recess!*
        *Joyful Parenting: Before You Blink They'll Be Grown*
Reality Therapy Certified

*Angering in the Family* by Dr. J. Thomas Bellows is a "must read" for professionals and laypersons alike. While written mostly from the perspective of domestic violence, Dr. Bellows' philosophy on living life through Choice Theory has tremendous application to all of us in the everyday choices we make. In an era regrettably punctuated by road rage, parking lot rage, relationship rage, instant gratification, and ever spiraling domestic violence, *Angering* provides a framework with which to gain insight into and change one's behavioral patterns while still meeting one's needs. Dr. Bellows is able to masterfully crochet theory into practical application, presenting anecdotal information evidence of the program's effectiveness. Having worked with Dr. Bellows professionally, I can attest to his commitment to his words. He practices what he preaches. His model for treatment in domestic violence cases should be a part of every therapist's treatment arsenal. As a psychologist, I wholeheartedly recommend *Angering in the Family* to all therapists and to anyone involved in a committed relationship."

> —**Andrew Yellen, Ph.D.**
> Licensed Clinical Psychologist
> Fellow and Diplomate of the Prescribing Psychologists' Register and the American Board of Medical Psychotherapists
> Lecturer on Behavioral Management, Attention-Deficit, Tourette Syndrome
> Educator with Standard Teaching, Community College, and Administrative Credentials
> Author: *The Art of Perfect Parenting and Other Absurd Ideas*
> *Social Facilitation in Action* (Co-authored with Illana Katz) *Understanding the Learning Disabled Athlete* (Co-authored with Heidi Yellen)

"In my twenty years in the domestic violence field and fifteen years of directing the Valley Center for the Prevention of Family Violence, I have not read a practical didactic and educational book like *Angering in the Family* by Dr. J. Thomas Bellows. Dr. Bellows' book clearly fills a gap in the existing literature on how to apply Choice Theory to stop family violence by perpetrators of Child Abuse and Domestic Violence. The creative approach of *Angering in the Family* gives us the hope that we have the choice in our hands to become better partners, parents, and human beings. Without any doubt, Dr. Bellows' book fulfills the needs of survival, love and belonging, fun, freedom and personal power the he clearly describes in his book."

> —**Virginia Baldioli, M.A.**
> Licensed Marriage, Family and Children Counselor
> Director, Valley Center for the Prevention of Family Violence

"J. Thomas Bellows, Ph.D. translates the essence of Choice Theory and Reality Therapy into practical strategies for family aggression. His suggestions in *Angering in the Family* range from negotiation of differences to personal responsibility and collaborative action plans. Dr. Bellows offers family members, counselors and law enforcement important tools and theory. Few professionals are willing to tackle the field of pervasive anger and anger management. When anger and control are the choice of behaving, victims feel powerless and frightened. Dr. Bellows provides techniques and guides to positive action and offers effective choices for both the abuser and the victim. This timeless and valuable contribution to the field of family violence will be on recommended reading lists for years."

  —Brandi Roth, Ph.D.
  Psychologist, Advocate and Lecturer in Beverly Hills, California
  Faculty member of The William Glasser Institute; Reality
  Therapy Certified and Basic Week Phase II Instructor Training
  Author: *Secrets to School Success* and *Choosing the Right School*
  Currently authoring: *Happy Ever After, A Couples Handbook*
  (co-author Clarann Goldring, Ph.D.)

# I

# CHOICE THEORY AND ANGERING

# 1

# Introduction

This book is the result of years of counseling domestic violence batterers, investigating child abuse allegations, attending conferences and other training sessions dealing with violence in the family. These experiences have taught me that it is the person and their individual choices that are responsible for the aggressive acts, not the other person's actions or life's circumstances that are responsible. The responsibility lies solely with the aggressor. These experiences have led me to believe that Choice Theory is a viable therapeutic model for counseling aggressive clients.

The purpose of this book is to demonstrate or explain a more appropriate method of relating to a spouse, mate, child or other significant person in one's life. Communication difficulties are worsened when one individual insists they are right and the other is wrong. Choice Theory teaches that the problem with which one struggles is usually not a simple issue of right and wrong. Oh how nice it would be if all of the choices in life were black or white, right or wrong.

Why is managing the choice to anger ("angering") so difficult? Angering is experienced more frequently than other emotions. Angering is as intense as fear and includes high sympathetic nervous system arousal. Angering lasts longer than other emotional states. Angering produces a strong tendency to approach, rather than avoid, the person or situation toward which your anger is directed. Angering includes an experience of greater power or potency than do the other emotions. Happiness is the only emotion people are less likely to want to change than angering.

The goal of this book is to illustrate that it is not the person or event that causes them to anger. Rather, it is how they choose their *total behavior* (how they think, act, feel, and their body physiology) regarding the person or event which leads to the choice to anger. Angering has many negative consequences because all of our total behavior is measured in the real world. Angering often leads to verbal and physical aggression and decreased problem solving. Non-angering total behavior leads to assertiveness and increased problem solving. When clients examine their choices to anger as a result of their beliefs and replace those choices with choices that bring them together with others instead of driving them away, they gain much happiness in their lives.

*It is not life's circumstances that make you angry. It is how you choose to totally behave about that circumstance that leads to your choice to anger.*

# Some of the Basics of Choice Theory

Happiness or mental health can be defined as enjoying the life you are choosing to live, getting along well with the people near and dear to you, doing something with your life you believe is worthwhile, and not doing anything to deprive anyone else of the same chance for the happiness that you have. Reality Therapy is used to help the client gain in his happiness and move into a state of mental health. Choice Theory is a way of living that illustrates how clients can live by use of caring habits instead of deadly habits and live in harmony with the other members of their family. This is different for clients who use anger and violence to gain control of the people around them and force their form of happiness on the family. We discuss solutions to the every day situations that arise in the member's lives and use the concepts of Choice Theory in arriving at non-violent behavior that will satisfy the needs of the person.

Choice Theory is the basis for all programs taught by the William Glasser Institute. It states that all we do is behave, that almost all behavior is chosen, and that we are driven by our genes to satisfy the fundamentals of human motivation—the five basic needs: *survival, love and belonging, power, freedom* and *fun*. The behavior is described as total behavior and consists of *acting, thinking, feelings,* and *physiology*.

In practice, the most important need is love and belonging, as closeness and connectedness with the people we care about is a requisite for satisfying all of our needs. Choice Theory is offered to replace external control psychology, the present psychology of almost all the people in the world.

The ten axioms of Choice Theory are:

1. The only person whose behavior we can control is our own. Control of another person is the crux of the domestic violence issue. We are responsible for what we do. If we really accept the idea that we choose our behavior and generate our emotional response, then we will not waste time and energy making excuses.

2. We are driven by five genetic needs: survival, love and belonging, power, freedom, and fun.

3. We can satisfy these needs only by satisfying a picture or pictures in our quality worlds. Of all we know, what we choose to put into our quality worlds is the most important.

4. All we can do from birth to death is behave: acting, thinking, feeling, and physiology.

5. All total behavior is designated by verbs, usually infinitives and gerunds, and named by the component that is most recognizable. The symptoms of anxiety, depression, and anger are emotional expressions of the total behavior that we generate. They are a part of a discouraged person's generated response, the attempt to gain a sense of inner control when the real world is perceived as disappointing. The external control culture tells us to think of these symptoms as conditions over which we have little or no control.

6. All total behavior is chosen, but we have direct control over only the acting and thinking components. The generated behavior elements are feeling and physiology. We always choose behavior for the purpose of meeting one of the five basic needs.

7. All we can give or get from other people is information. How we deal with that information is our or their choice.

8. All long-lasting psychological problems are relationship problems.

9. The problem relationship is always part of our present lives.

10. What happened in the past that was painful has a great deal to do with what we are today, but revisiting this painful past can contribute little or nothing to what we need to do now: improve an important, present relationship.

Choice Theory suggests that the partners can bring about a positive present relationship by using the *"seven caring habits,"* i.e. *supporting, encouraging, listening, accepting, trusting, respecting,* and *negotiating the differences.* These are differentiated from the "seven deadly habits" that will get in the way of a positive relationship and bring frustration and anger into the relationship, i.e. *criticizing, blaming, complaining, nagging, threatening, punishing,* and *bribing to control.*

HOW THE BRAIN WORKS (*Chart Talk*), was created by William Glasser as a description of the interactions of the brain and his concept of Choice Theory. This author has found that, in group work with domestic violence aggressors, the simplified version of the chart given in Chapter 2 of this book is adequate to bring to recall the details of the full chart. The simplified version facilitates the use of the clients' own events in place of the description of the theory and personalizes the counseling.

# Angering

## Frustration

- The emotion humans experience when they do not get what they think they should or must get, or when they are denied that to which they believe they are entitled.

- The emotion humans experience when they are starkly confronted by the realization that they cannot control others.

- The emotion that activates the sympathetic nervous system, physiology (e.g., increasing heart rate, increasing muscle tension, etc) results in a significantly increased likelihood of aggressive behavior and results in seriously diminished problem solving, parenting skills and interpersonal relationships.

- The emotion humans experience when they do not get what they prefer, desire, hope, want or wish for.

- Leads to angering as a choice of total behavior.

# Where does anger come from?

The things we would like, wish, hope, and prefer to have turn into things we believe we must, should, ought to, are entitled to, and demand to have. Would our life be easier, better, and more pleasant if we got everything we thought we should? YES! But is that the real world in which we live? NO! The important thing to remember is that it is not written anywhere (except in our head) that others must, or must not, do anything.

**Entitlement.** To believe that we are entitled to something means that it is 'due' or 'owed' to us. Examples: "I'm entitled to be treated fairly at all times." "I'm entitled to have a good paying job." "I'm entitled to be taken care of by others." "I'm entitled to have what I want, when I want it." These are true only if "I were God and ruled the world then I'd make it that way."

**Control.** When others do not do what we think they should, we choose angering. You may have successfully controlled others in the past when you were a child and your parents gave in to your angering actions. But, there are at least three problems with believing that your angering is capable of controlling others. First it overlooks the fact that others have freedom of choice and that their compliance with your demand is not because you made them do anything but rather it represents a decision to comply on their part. Second, simply because someone chooses to give in to your angry demands today, it does not mean that they will do so tomorrow. And, third, when others perceive that we are trying to control them, they often chose to behave the exact opposite of what we are demanding and commanding of them.

**Fantasy.** Angering is a product of living in the world of 'should' where things are perfectly right for you. They are perfect because they are exactly the way you think they should, must, and ought to be. You always get what you want, when you want it, without delay or interference for others. Hard work is always rewarded. People never lie or gossip. Parents love and support their children, and children love and obey their parents.

The real world is different than the ideal world. Life is not always fair. You treat people well but they do not always treat you well back. You work hard and have to wait for any kind of reward. Bad things sometimes do happen to good people.

**Shame.** Shame is the result of a strong sense of guilt, embarrassment or disgrace. "We think that we did something wrong." Shame is what we feel when our inappropriate behavior is uncovered and made available for all to see. It is the emotion we experience when we are laid bare psychologically as the world passes judgment on the choices we have made. Rather than experience shame, some individuals choose to transform the emotion into anger. This angering, often directed towards those who have discovered them, allows them to feel powerful and potent again, where once their shame had made them feel powerless.

## The lies we tell ourselves to justify our anger

### Lie #1: "If I do not get angry, and behave aggressively, people will think I'm a wimp and walk all over me."

Many people rely on angering, and then act aggressively, as a way of countering the perceptions of others, that they are weak. The problem with this approach is that, if someone is determined to view you as weak, all the anger and aggression you can generate will not necessarily change his or her view of you. As a matter of fact, others will actually point to your anger as proof that you are weak and out of control. As you will learn, being able to choose your total behavior, including ones other than anger, are signs of strength, not weakness.

### Lie #2: "I just get angry. Emotions are things over which I have no control."

The notion of being able to choose your emotional response in a particular situation at first sounds strange. Throughout our lives we have been taught that emotions are things that happen to us and, as such, are beyond our control. Nothing, however, could be further from the truth. Emotions, as you will learn, are products of how you think and act in specific situations. To the extent that you control your thoughts and actions, so, too, can you exercise control over your emotions as part of your total behavior.

### Lie #3: "Only by expressing my anger am I going to feel better. I should never keep my anger bottled up."

While people who chronically choose to anger are more likely to experience certain physical problems than their counterparts who do not choose to anger, that does not mean that the solution to your anger problem involves spewing anger out every time you experience it. The reality is that there are countless examples of people you are better off not expressing anger towards, such as spouses, children, police officers, employers, judges and gangsters brandishing guns. Rather that struggling not to act out your angering, or surrendering to it by acting it out, you need to learn to manage your anger to avoid both the physical problems associated with its repression as well as the personal and interpersonal problems associated with its expression.

## Lie #4: "There is no such thing as healthy anger."

As with other negative emotional choices (i.e., to depress or to elevate your levels of anxiety), angering can be viewed as conveying information concerning the current state of one's perceived world as compared with one's quality world. Anger can alert you to problems in your comparing place that need to be solved. Used in this way, angering can be helpful and in that respect, healthy. People who use Choice Theory use their angering this way. Others, instead, believe that there is such a thing as healthy irritation that helps you overcome life's problems, while intense feelings of anger will always cause you more problems. This is a partial solution, but choice theory can bring more happiness to the person who lives by its concepts.

## Lie #5: "Hitting something, like a pillow, will help me deal better with my anger."

There is no evidence to support the value of 'letting off steam' as the best way to deal with anger. Evidence supports that this is the wrong way to learn angering control. In the case of hitting a pillow, you will feel better immediately after discharging your anger. Unfortunately, rather than dealing with your anger in constructive ways, you are simply rehearsing future aggressive behaviors. In cases like this, the person recalls the momentary relief they experience after behaving aggressively. That split-second of relief reinforces their aggressive behavior, and as a consequence, they tend to behave this way in the future. This sense of immediate relief is also easily transferable from hitting inanimate objects to hitting people.

## Lie #6: "I cannot help it if other people, or situations, make me angry."

This is the greatest lie of all. How many times have you said to yourself, "(Fill in the blank) makes me so angry!" or "I would not have gotten angry if (fill in the blank) had done what he said he would do!" Do you see any problems with believing that other people make you angry? As long as you believe that other people make you angry, they are in control of your emotions! As long as you believe that other people make you angry, you are powerless over your anger!

To be in control of your total behavior, to regain your personal power, it is essential that you abandon the notion that others *make* you angry and replace it with the proposition that only you are powerful enough to choose your own feelings and how to deal with them.

## To where (or To what end) does angering lead?

**Angering can kill you.** Research clearly demonstrates that persons unable to manage their angering are at greater risk for heart disease, high blood pressure, headaches, strokes and stomach-related problems. Studies suggest that persons reporting higher levels of angering at age twenty-five are four to seven times more likely to be dead by age fifty than those persons reporting lower levels of angering.

**Angering destroys your most important relationships.** No one enjoys being around a person when they are angering. Like the other deadly habits, angering pushes others away, isolating you from them and from the world.

**Society punishes people who anger and act aggressively.** If you are unable to manage your anger, and the aggressive actions growing out of that anger, society, through its legal mechanisms, will attempt to control your actions for you—most likely in ways you will not like. No matter how self-righteous or justified you might believe your anger to be, society will punish you, especially if your anger turns into aggression.

**Life will find ways to punish you for your angry actions.** This is a somewhat philosophical observation but one that angry people understand almost immediately. Opportunities that may have materialized, had you been less aggressive, pass you by. Doors that may have opened, because of your skills or knowledge, remain closed because others fear being exposed to your excessive aggression.

Angering leads to decreased problem solving. Angering leads to verbal and physical aggression. There are three forms of angering.

**Passive:** Passive behaviors are the opposite of aggressive behaviors. Instead of harming others, either physical or verbally, we allow others to run us over without protesting. Instead of stating our thoughts, feelings and wishes we remain silent and allow others to push us around.

**Passive-aggressive:** Passive-aggressive behaviors involve an indirect expression of anger. Rather than coming out and saying that we are angry, we let people know through your tone of voice and other behaviors such as sulking, pouting or giving someone the cold shoulder or silent treatment.

**Aggression:** Aggressive behaviors include hitting things, hitting other people, verbally beating other people up and threatening people. They are designed to intimidate and control others by force, regardless of the costs. When we choose aggression, we are likely to speak in a loud voice and get up in the other person's face while making our demands.

"Domestic violence is not simply a private family matter—it is a matter affecting the entire community. Too many of America's homes have become places where *women, children, and seniors suffer physical abuse and emotional trauma.* Domestic violence is a leading cause of injury to women in our country, and it occurs among all racial, ethnic, religious, and economic groups. It is a particularly devastating form of abuse because it wears a familiar face: the face of a spouse, parent, partner or child. This violence too often extends beyond the home and into the workplace."—President Clinton's proclamation of National Domestic Violence Awareness Month, October 1, 1997. (Italics added by author to indicate an implied definition of "domestic violence" that involves the entire family.)

Between three and ten million children in the USA each year, observe abuse of one parent by the other. Violence in the family is a major contributor to abuse of children. 100% of the children in a violent family are aware of the violence and are affected in some manner. Understanding the aspects of violence in the family can reduce or possibly eliminate this abuse. Additionally, peace and stability can be enjoyed by all members of the family, fostering a more calm and safe home environment. If the aspects of violence in the family can be understood and reduced or eliminated, then peace and stability can be provided for the children of the family.

Aggressive behavior is the hallmark of "external control psychology". It represents an attempt to solve problems by imposing one's will on others and pressuring them to do what you want. Aggression is satisfying because it produces a measure of power in the experience of the offender. However, it is only marginally satisfying because aggression separates the parties from one another and love and belonging suffer from the separation. Marginally satisfying aggressive behavior usually progresses to more serious levels. What begins as a hostile or threatening attitude develops into overtly abusive behavior with time.

In homes where domestic violence or family aggression occurs between partners, children are at high risk of suffering physical abuse themselves. They, themselves, learn that aggression is the solution to many of their problems and becomes a need satisfying behavior for them. The American Humane Society (1994) found that women who have been beaten by their spouses are twice as likely as other women to abuse a child. Regardless of whether children are physically abused, the emotional effects of witnessing domestic violence are very similar to the psychological trauma associated with being a victim of child abuse. Children in homes where domestic violence occurs are physically abused or seriously neglected at a rate of 1500% higher than the average in the general population (Center For The Prevention of Domestic Violence, 1997). Donna Wills, Chief District Attorney of the Los Angeles County Family Violence Unit, reports that 90% of all death row offenders allege domestic violence or child abuse in their background (Wills, 1995). The California State Child Abuse Laws (Welfare & Institutions Code 300) allow for the removal of children from a domestically violent home based on the assumption that the children will experience emotional abuse and be at high risk of physical abuse due to the violence.

A comparison of delinquent and non-delinquent youth revealed a history of family violence or abuse is the most significant difference between the two groups.

Aggression in the family or domestic violence is a major problem in our society today. In a national survey of over 6,000 American families, 50 percent of the men who frequently assaulted their wives also frequently abused their children. More children are served in battered women's shelters than are adults. Children are present in more than half of the homes where police are called for domestic violence.

Counseling aggressive people with external control methods is like using force to deal with force and can lead to more anger within the aggressor. The courts order the clients to come to counseling to learn how to live without angering and violence. As a result to these orders, the clients are usually angry at the courts and resent having to be in the group. This further perpetuates their resentment of external control and the system. They arrive blaming the partner, law enforcement, the District Attorney, the Public Defender, the Court and anyone else they can blame—everyone except themselves.

There are three categories of aggressors; "family only", "generally violent" and "emotionally volatile." The "family only" aggressors are least likely to be violent outside the home. The "generally violent" aggressors are most likely to be violent outside the home. And, the "emotionally volatile" aggressors are angry, depressed and jealous; exhibit some physical violence and much psychological abuse.

Common characteristics of all abusers:

- use of projection (blaming the mate for the marital strife),
- disallow mate's autonomy (mate can only be a possession or an extension of their ego),
- mate is a symbol (mate is not a person but a symbol of someone or something else),
- mate adheres to expectations of marriage (demands that both adhere to the aggressor's original expectation of what a marriage is like),
- have attractive characteristics (no one is totally evil or vicious), and
- lack of intimacy (unable to attain the mutuality of a truly intimate relationship).

The power and control wheel from Power and Control by E. Pence and M. Paymar, 1986, shows how abusive partners use different forms of sexual, social and psychological abuse to maintain power and control. Once this pattern has begun, it will cycle around again until the threat of physical abuse begins to overshadow all aspects of a battered woman's life. The wheel contains eight elements.

## ISOLATION

Controlling what she does, who she sees and talks to, where she goes.

## EMOTIONAL ABUSE

Pulling her down or making her feel bad about herself. Calling her names. Making her think she's crazy. Mind games.

## INTIMIDATION

Fuming her in fear by: using looks, actions, gestures, loud voice, smashing things, destroying her property.

## ECONOMIC ABUSE

Trying to keep her from getting or keeping a job. Making her ask for money. Giving her an allowance. Taking her money.

## USING MALE PRIVELEGE

Treating her like a servant. Making all the "big" decisions. Acting like the "master of the castle."

## SEXUAL ABUSE

Making her do sexual things against her will. Physically attacking the sexual parts of her body. Treating her like a sex object.

## THREATS

Making and/or carrying out threats to do something to hurt her emotionally. Threaten to take the children, commit suicide, and report her to welfare.

## USING CHILDREN

Making her feel guilty about the children. Using the children to give messages. Using visitation as a way lo harass her.

These elements lead to pushing, shoving, hitting, slapping, choking, pulling hair, twisting arms, tripping, biting, beating, throwing her down, using a weapon against her, punching kicking and grabbing that are all forms of *physical abuse*.

Additional characteristics of the aggressor include:

- jealousy,
- controlling behavior,
- a short engagement or relationship before moving in with a mate or partner,
- non-realistic expectations of the relationship,
- accuses others for their own problems and feelings,
- supersensitive,
- verbally abusive, and
- makes threats of physical violence toward the mate, family, and others.

Children of battering families are physically abused and neglected at the rate of up to 15 times higher than the national average. Their brains form differently than children who grow up in families that are not anger driven. They learn that the world is not a safe place to live and not to trust anyone. In addition to any physical or sexual abuse children may be subjected to, they are aware of the violence directed at their parent(s). The tension in the home results in poor schooling and other areas of neglect. Children who witness abuse of their caretaker were 24 times more likely to commit sexual assault crimes; 50 percent more likely to abuse drugs and/or alcohol; 74 percent more likely to commit crimes against another person; and six times more likely to commit suicide.

Angering leads to punishment.

Self-discipline or self-control is a term that we use daily and think that we understand. The roots of the word discipline are found in the word disciple. To be a disciple means to be "One who embraces and assists in spreading the teaching of another." Thus, to be a disciple means not only to be a kind of follower, but also to be a teacher. I consider myself to be a disciple of Choice Theory. Self-control is a form of self-teaching or self-instruction or self-regulation. For most of us, the first disciples or teachers in our lives are our parents.

Parents need to first instruct themselves in self-control before attempting to instruct their children in self-control. How many parents do you know who demonstrate self-control? Do *you* operate from a position of self-control? How many parents believe that they are capable of disciplining their children when they are themselves undisciplined?

When we are having difficulty with our children, the first place we need to look for answers is in the mirror. Rather than focusing our energy on trying to change or control them, look to see how we can change ourselves. If we cannot manage ourselves, how can we teach our children to manage themselves? When we are managing our anger, we are practicing self-control. Children see this self-control, respect it, and seek to emulate us. Once we have disciplined ourselves, only then are we ready to discipline our children.

A relationship exists between anger and poor parenting skills (i.e., external control or relying primarily on punishment as the means of getting children to alter their behavior). A similar relationship exists between control theory and improved parenting skills (i.e., relying primarily on the relationship with your children as the means of influencing children to make the choice to alter their behavior). Influencing children is not the same as punishing them. Punishment is a behavior growing out of anger. It is designed solely to reduce the likelihood of certain behaviors, with which you, as a parent do not agree, from occurring in the future. When we are angry, and thinking only of punishing our child, we deprive them of the opportunity to learn as much as they can from their experiences. Helping them learn from their experiences and influencing them from our behavior are goals of choice theory parenting.

Children who learn to accept violence as a means of conflict resolution often fail to develop their own inner controls. They learn to maintain control of others by using threats of violence. They learn that loved ones have the right to hurt one another. They often feel guilty for the violence between their parents or for the violence toward themselves. They feel angry toward one or both parents. They experience anxiety and fear. They often "protect" the abuser in the face of outside intervention. They have sleep disturbances such as bed-wetting, nightmares, and insomnia. They have difficulties in school such as staying awake, concentrating on work, and playing with peers. These children are often diagnosed with ADHD or ADD and medicated. They have poor appetites. They often confuse love with violence. They learn unhealthy sex-role stereotypes from their parents. And they grow up to be abusers of their own mates and children.

Parenting is not an easy job. It takes patience, creativity, an endless amount of love and understanding. Some parenting skills come naturally; however, many need to be learned. The same can be said of being a child. Their curiosity is natural; however, self discipline must be learned. As parents, we are responsible for teaching self discipline to our children. It takes time and practice—but it does get easier—as children learn to control their behavior. It does not have to hurt us or our child(ren). Chapter 4, *Helping Children Become Adults—Parenting* is included in this book to address violence and discipline in the family. Much of the violence is aggression in the name of influence or discipline. This book does not go into parenting techniques in additional detail because this book is intended to provide the underlying philosophy that will make those techniques useful and successful. The reader is referred to the totality of parenting books and articles currently in publication.

# Can abusers be cured, or must they be punished?

There is a quiet battle brewing among those who work with batterers over what type of treatment will best protect the victims of family violence. This treatment debate stems from a deeper schism over what makes batterers tick.

On one side is the pro-feminist approach—maintain that family abuse is the product of a sexist society that accepts male dominance over women. Many men have been taught to view women as sex objects—a woman is a man's property and that it is both their right and their duty as men to dominate. Men do not respect women and what needs to change is that sense of entitlement—that it is their right to control the lives of their partners. Battering is not a sickness, it's a learned behavior. Following this line of reasoning, the pro-feminists view power and control as the driving force behind domestic violence. Batterers are control freaks who consciously manipulate their partners to ensure they get their way. They need to be told how to act or be thrown in jail.

On the other side of the debate is the psychological model. This side believes that violence stems from deep character flaws created by traumatic childhood experiences and stunted character development. Following this line of thinking, the best way to protect women is to explore, and ultimately change, the glaring character defects that drive the abuser. At the core of this treatment battle is a debate over whether batterers can change.

Based on their belief that batterers are fundamentally controlling, calculating, manipulative people, the pro-feminist thinkers believe this is a pie-in-the-sky hope. As a result, these pro-feminist/behavior modification programs employ a social control approach to batterers' treatment that focuses almost exclusively on the here and now. Group leaders confront the batterers, forcing them to accept responsibility for their actions. They are not allowed to blame their behavior on their partner, alcohol, the economy, their temper, their childhood or any other excuse. They did it, there was no excuse—and they will either stop or be put in jail. Group members explore the attitudes toward women they use to justify their abuse. They learn ways to control their anger, and communicate more effectively with their partner. They learn that abuse is not just beatings, but also threats, insults, psychological abuse and economic control.

There has been an ongoing debate between the psychological and the confrontational, external control, approach and there still is not any conclusion. But there is no doubt that men who come to batterer programs are like long-term alcoholics—they've developed tremendous systems of rationalization and denial and need a forceful and consistent message. The more you diffuse that message with psychology, the more it feeds into their rationalization. The sooner they accept responsibility for their behavior, the sooner that their victims will be safe.

Richard Gelles, a nationally recognized domestic violence researcher at the University of Rhode Island, said there is no evidence that the confrontational method works best in all cases. Belief that it does is based more on what makes the treatment professional feel good than on any empirical evidence that it has the best results.

While incorporating many of the principles and methods developed in the pro-feminist approach, proponents of the psychological model believe the only way to protect women is to help the men change. They believe that if you want to make the effects of treatment last, you've got to make these men change from the inside out. If all you do is threaten them with the court and jail, it will not last. The pro-feminist view all batterers as calculating criminals.

The model that is described in this book combines the pro-feminist and the psychological models and addresses their elements through using Choice Theory. It teaches the batterers that they cannot control others, that they are responsible for all of their total behavior, and that external control can be replaced by internal control (Choice Theory) that will bring them happiness in their present relationships.

Most of these men are not proud of what they're doing and a lot of their resistance to treatment is in not wanting to face the shame. We try to foster pride in dealing with a situation in a way that shows respect for the partner and stresses their responsibility for their total behavior. A large portion of the program is spent helping batterers build their ability to make better decisions and use the caring habits instead of the deadly habits.

Those who favor the pro-feminist/behavioral approach contend that allowing batterers to explore their inner wounds undermines the hard-won gains of the first half of the treatment. Choice Theory believes that the pain that happened in the past has a great deal to do with who we are today, however revisiting the past pain can contribute little or nothing to what we need to do now: improve an important, present relationship. This is a behavioral education program that teaches Choice Theory to the client.

There is no research to support the notion that short-term therapy works. The 52 weeks of the mandated program is long enough for all but the most ingrained men to endorse and begin to use the tenets of Choice Theory. There are only a small percentage of the men coming through the program that are the macho control freaks who are unable to make the choice to change their behavior and improve their happiness through an improved important relationship. This program teaches the client how to make such a change.

# Requirements to Close a Court Case

When aggression comes to the attention of the courts, the following conditions are considered by the court prior to deciding on the need for further counseling or case closure. The court uses the word "defendant" to identify the "primary aggressor" who was established by law enforcement investigation. The primary aggressor is the person who elevated the violence to a level intended to control the other person. This does not mean that the partner was not also an aggressor, but the partner is considered the "victim" by the courts. The defendant is often the male aggressor in the relationship because the male is the one who is able to elevate the level of physical violence to one that could be used to control the behavior of his partner. Or, in other words, the male is the one who can overpower the partner in most relationships.

There are eight stated requirements to close a case in the courts of California. They are:

1. The defendant has been violence free for a minimum of one year. This includes all forms of violence including violence outside of an intimate relationship.

2. The defendant has cooperated and participated in the batterer's program.

3. The defendant demonstrates an understanding of and practices positive conflict resolution skills.

4. The defendant does not blame, degrade or has not committed acts that dehumanize the victim or puts the victim's safety at risk.

5. The defendant understands that the use of coercion or violent behavior to maintain dominance is unacceptable in an intimate relationship.

6. The defendant has not made threats to harm anyone in any manner. Again this includes behavior outside of the intimate relationship.

7. The defendant has complied with applicable requirements to receive alcohol and/or drug counseling.

8. The defendant demonstrates acceptance of responsibility for the abusive behavior perpetrated against the victim.

Rachor (1995) used self-reports from both men and women to evaluate the first step in the Passages Domestic Violence Program. Even though the study was flawed by inadequate controls as well as participants underreporting their aggression, the study still showed notable results. Comparable studies cited by Rachor indicated that many other treatment programs seldom made any difference in recidivism, while some studies indicated modest decreases in violence.

The clients, men and women, participated in a 21-session program, subdivided into two phases, with each session lasting 2 ½ hours in length. The first phase dealt with the application of control theory (Choice Theory) and reality therapy to domestic violence as well as the roots of domestic violence, cycles of violence, and related topics. The second phase consisted of applying the techniques to the family as units, to help children. For example, developing an internal locus of control and encouraging all family members to spend quality time in relationships.

This survey research included 45 clients (23 females and 22 males) who were selected randomly. Participants answered open-ended questions via telephone interviews conducted by trained volunteers. The answers were analyzed and grouped under descriptive headings.

Two-thirds of the males reported they learned better self-control and 40 percent of the women indicated increased self-confidence and self-esteem as well as the ability to relinquish attempts to control others. Continued threats of violence were reported by only 17 percent of females, including 13 percent indicating multiple acts of violence.

Currently California requires 104 hours of mandatory group time with the aggressor and has an additional free optional program for the victim. There is no provision for the family to deal with the issues that are the basis for the frustration in the relationship or the effects on the children from the union. This author does not know of any studies that have been conducted on the effectiveness of the current California requirements or the use of Choice Theory in a program to accomplish the requirements to close a case. This author has had no clients return to his program due to additional violence in the home since initiating the Choice Theory model into his program.

Reality therapy and Choice Theory as described by Dr. William Glasser in his book *Choice Theory* (1998) allows the aggressor to change the anger into productive choices from destructive choices that are directed against the victims or society. Choice Theory states that we choose our total behavior to fulfill one or more of the basic needs that are a construct of our genetic and our psychological structure. A program using Choice Theory can satisfy all of the requirements listed above so that the court can close the case.

Choice Theory explains the whole mechanism of genetic needs, the symptoms associated with their frustration, and the choices of behavior people make while experiencing their frustration.

The aggressors are responsible for their total behavior—**thinking, acting, feeling,** and **physiology.** All we can do is give information to others. We explain to the clients that the heart of Reality Therapy and Choice Theory is the message: *The behavior we choose in a relationship, not what the behavior chosen for us or by us for others, is the heart of living happily with another person.*

The facilitator helps the client relate to the individuals in the group as well as to the facilitator. The client can choose to use what he learns with the group and begin to relate more effectively to the other people in his life. The facilitator's interactions set the example so that the client learns how to behave with others by imitating the facilitator's actions, words, and the manner in which he relates to each of the members of the group.

When there is difficulty in any relationship, it is caused by one or both of the parties using external power and control. When we replace that external control with Choice Theory, life will improve. Using Choice Theory in an external control environment—court ordered mandatory attendance—is a challenging endeavor, but one which can bring great rewards to the family and the community.

# 2

# Discussion

The diagram below explains in Choice Theory terms how the brain works and why we behave as we do. It was developed from a more comprehensive chart developed by Dr. William Glasser and presented in *Chart Talk* (2000). The workbook explains the chart that *The William Glasser Institute* published to illustrate how the brain works and why and how we behave. The explanation emphasizes how Choice Theory is used both to counsel and/or to manage people. This simplified chart is used as a short hand reference for the group members who are familiar with the elements of Choice Theory so that they can put the discussion in perspective and relate it to the overall theory. Often, during group discussions, the group refers to the elements of the chart, to obtain clarity of understanding the relationship of events to Choice Theory concepts.

**CHOICE THEORY – WHY AND HOW WE BEHAVE**

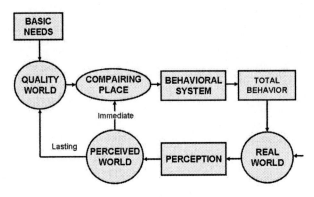

Reality therapy, based on Choice Theory, is a unique counseling method. The following eight tenants explain Choice Theory and are used in counseling aggressors.

1. People choose the total behavior that has led them into domestic violence because it is their best effort to deal with a present, unsatisfying relationship.

2. The facilitator helps clients choose new relationship-improving behaviors that are more effective in satisfying one or more of their basic needs.

3. We must perceive that we have good relationships with other people to satisfy all of our basic needs. (*Satisfying the need for love and belonging while not giving up the need for power is the key to satisfying the all five basic needs.*)

4. Reality therapy focuses on the here and now instead of past events because *love and belonging can only be satisfied in the present.*

5. The solution to our problems is rarely found in the discussions of the past unless the focus is on past successes and not failures.

6. Focusing on the current symptoms avoids the real problem of *improving present relationships.*

7. The continuing goal of reality therapy is to create a Choice Theory relationship between the client and the facilitator as well as the individuals in the group. The facilitator models the relationship with the client and thus sets an example of how this is accomplished.

8. Understanding and practicing Choice Theory is an integral part of practicing reality therapy. The clients are encouraged to integrate this into their lives and relationships.

Reality therapy gets to the root of the actual problem—improving a present relationship or finding a new, more satisfying one. Diagnostic labels, brain drugs and dreams are not used in reality therapy. People with conditions of mental illness, such as Alzheimer's disease, epilepsy, head trauma and brain infections, as well as genetic defects, such as Down's syndrome, Huntington's chorea, and autism should be treated primarily by neurologists instead of counselors or facilitators. Glasser does not label people as having a mental illness unless there is pathology in the brain. *Psychiatric symptoms are a person's current best attempt to regain inner control and emotional balance.*

## Amond's Story

*Dr. Amond is a medical doctor who was sentenced to the domestic class for disturbing the peace. His fiancé accused him of hitting her in the mouth and the judge determined that she was lying. Dr. Amond resigned himself to attending the classes and decided to get the most out of them. When I introduced the concept that brain drugs were not a part of Choice Theory, he took exception to it and questioned me. I suggested that he read the book,* Warning: Psychiatry Can Be Hazardous To Your Mental Health *by Dr. William Glasser and gave him a copy.*

*Dr. Amond read the book and reported in class that the book made some very valid points and that he was re-thinking his position. Medicine may be helpful in the beginning treatment of some of the behaviors associated with unhappiness, but in the long term, regaining one's happiness was not necessarily dependent on the continued use of the drugs. Dr. Amond asked his mother, who was a teacher, to read the book and she supported his conclusions. He then asked his sister, who is a psychiatrist, to read the book. She said she was very familiar with Dr. Glasser's work and agreed with him that brain drugs were not necessary when treating the unhappiness caused by poor relationships.*

*Dr. Amond reports that since his investigation into the subject, he has reduced the prescribing of brain drugs by 70% with no noticeable adverse effects on his patients. He admits that some of his colleagues prescribe medication so their patients will become dependent upon them for the prescription renewal appointments that provide a continuing income.*

Many clients come to the group choosing to depress or to anger, and many of those are often treated with medication. These clients are discovering when they begin to make healthier choices in dealing with the problems in their life and improve their important relationships; the medication is no longer needed. Their doctors reduce and/or completely eliminate their need for medication.

## Total Behavior

Dr. Glasser defines all behavior as total behavior. Choice Theory explains that all behavior is composed of four distinct yet inseparable components: *acting, thinking, feeling,* and the *physiology* that accompanies the other three. That is why it is called Total Behavior. We choose our total behavior and when it resembles someone else's behavior the Diagnostic and Statistics Manual of Mental Disorders (4th Ed) categorizes, groups and, labels it. The courts have done the same thing by calling it Domestic Violence or battery to a domestic partner in a domestic setting. Actions and thoughts are clearly cognitive behaviors and if we wish to change our total behavior, we must change the way we act and think. When the actions and thoughts are changed, the way we feel about things, even our physical being is also changed. When we solve a problem, our stress is reduced, we can sleep better and as a result we feel better. The physical symptoms associated with the problem have been changed and we just feel better. Thinking and acting are the elements of the total behavior that we use to satisfy our basic needs because they are the only components we can directly control. None of us can wish the past away. All we can do is control our own present total behavior.

The first step in dealing with the domestic violence that was committed is for the aggressor to take responsibility for the choices used. These choices started with the frustration that was felt and resulted in violence as defined by the law. These choices involve all four of the elements of total behavior. Acting out the lack of situational control was the violent behavior and the thinking was "I need to control this situation." The feeling was one of frustration because events were not going as the aggressor wanted. The physiology element was most likely present in the elevated heart rate and faster breathing that accompanies most aggressive actions.

In one discussion of total behavior, a group member questioned the statement that "we always take the best choice of action at the time we make the choice." A few minutes later, the choice we made earlier may turn out to be a poor choice; but at the time we made it, we thought it was the best available action to make. When I stated, "No one intentionally makes a bad choice." the client agreed with the original statement about always making the best choice. *It is difficult for the aggressor to see that using force is what they thought was the best choice for them at the time they made the choice.*

Throughout the classes, clients begin to see how they could have made better choices. They begin to practice making better choices in their lives. Clients begin to learn that they had other choices at the time of their violence. As they learn about Choice Theory and their possible choices, their behavioral system expands to include many of these different choices.

# Juan's Story

*Juan was ordered by the judge to attend domestic violence class for being violent with his wife. He reported that he saw neighbors fighting. The husband was beating up his wife in the common area of the apartments. Juan stated that he got dressed and went outside to break up the fight. By the time he got there, the wife was bloody; lying on the ground and the husband was still hitting her. Juan stepped between the two with his arms folded over his chest so as not to become a fighter himself. Juan just stayed between the two until the police arrived. The man hit Juan several times as the man attempted to continue the fight with his wife. The responding police officers consisted of a lead female officer and a male supporting officer. The male officer's questioning revealed that all parties reported that Juan had stepped between the husband and wife to break up the fight and was not a party to the fight himself. The male officer told this to the female officer. The female officer asked Juan if he was on probation and Juan answered truthfully that he was on probation. The female officer checked his record and found that he had been convicted of domestic violence in the past and then she made the decision to take Juan to the station along with the other two people. Juan spent 2 nights in jail before going before a judge. After hearing the story from all three, the judge determined that Juan had not committed any crime, but instead was trying to protect the female of the couple. The judge released Juan immediately.*

*After additional deliberation, Juan stated that he was responding to a principle in his quality world that stated that it was not correct for a man to hit a woman. He perceived that he could intervene and stop this injustice. He stated that he was anxious and that his heart was racing. He stated that his total behavior was "reacting to the situation" without thinking about the elements and consequences. The reactions were based on his past learning in his behavioral system. He did not think much about the situation before acting. Juan came to the conclusion that calling 911 on his cell phone or his cordless phone while he was walking toward the couple might have been a better choice. This would have provided some witness to his story. Calling 911 would have provided contact with the police prior to their arrival, and would have established his intentions and actions before his previous domestic violence arrest became an overriding factor. Still, Juan was thinking about imposing external control on the situation instead of giving the couple their own choice as to their behavior.*

Additional review of the incident might include asking some additional questions as part of the thinking process of total behavior and reality therapy. Who was Juan trying to control and why was he trying to control the situation? What was in his quality world that was driving his desire to control the situation? What was his total behavior before he made the choice to intervene? What were his actions, feelings, physiology, and thoughts? Did the past behavioral system drive the feelings, physiology, and actions leaving the thinking element behind? What other actions might have kept Juan from being taken to jail and still satisfy his basic needs and quality world? How could he participate in the situation without trying to externally control others? How would the situation look to the police officers when they arrived and conducted the limited amount of investigation before arresting all three parties? What did he perceive in the real world that put his comparison between his perceived world and his quality world so out of balance that he thought it required the ineffective intervention?

# Relationship

The second step in dealing with the client and their partner is their relationship. It must be evaluated if the relationship is to continue as a love and belonging relationship. The aggressive act might have been the terminating incident and the parties are going to separate. If there are children as a result of this relationship, the problem involves more than the two partners. If this continuing relationship is one of aggression, Dr. Glasser believes there will be long-lasting psychological problems. These problems will always be a part of the family's present lives.

As domestic violence groups deal only with the aggressor, the statement of the ongoing relationship is a one-sided opinion. Only time in the group will reveal the reality of this opinion. The client is the only reporter of what is wrong with the relationship. Usually the client starts out using external control by saying they were aggressive because the partner made them aggressive and they were only trying to get away from the fight. The Choice Theory education process begins with this report of the incident. Most of the time, the other members of the group who have learned about Choice Theory confront the new member by asking if the partner controls the client or does the client control the partner. They, then, explain to the new client that they control themselves and that they cannot control their partners, nor can the partners control the client. Therefore, the client is responsible for choosing to act aggressively. It will take several sessions for the new clients to start to understand this principal and more time to accept it for themselves.

In the groups, I ask a new client to explain why they stay with their partner. What is good about the relationship right now? Much of the time, the answer is the sex. Another often used answer is that they stay because of the child or children. Other people think, "I am special because she is a real babe." Alternatively, "I am a real stud." Seldom does the client state that they are still in love with their partner and that they want to change their lives so that they can make the relationship work better. Some say that they are willing to change their way of relating to others, but most of the clients say that they are not willing to change first. They say: "Why do I have to do all of the changing and she does not have to do any. It is not fair." There is a county fair in Pomona, California, near Los Angeles, and when the clients say that something is not "fair," I respond that "fair" only occurs in Pomona. This group is for them to learn how to live a life of better choices and not even things out for their poor choices. Only they can be in charge of their own choices. "Fairness" does not play a part in their learning how to make better choices in life.

The clients do not know what they can do to make their relationships better. They think that all they have to do is find the "right partner." A partner who will behave in the manner that they want and treat them the way they want to be treated. Most clients are afraid that their existing partner or a new partner will report them to the police for "false" charges and view this fear as external control. They think that once they have a record, that the police will arrest them without listening to them. This is often true and sometimes the police give the female partners the advantage by arresting the male without doing a thorough investigation. This is especially true if the male has a previous record of domestic violence. One of the things that the client has to learn is that in selecting a new partner, they should look for one who has learned and uses Choice Theory in their life. If they do, then they stand a great chance of having a satisfying relationship and can free from the fear of being reported for "false" charges. Without Choice Theory, the relationship suffers from the constant trying to force the partner to be different or to punish each other for real or perceived wrongs that cause most of the problems. This external control poisons every relationship in which it is used.

## Al's Story

*Al has contended he did not assault his wife and that she falsely accused him of hitting her. He is now in the process of finalizing the custody arrangements of their two children. He had full custody of them for the past few years, but when he wanted to move back to his hometown in the East, he made a temporary custody agreement with their mother to have custody of them until he found a permanent situation. Once settled, he then planned to return to California and move the children to his new home. The move did not work out and when Al came back to California, the children's mother would not return the children to him.*

*Al knew about Choice Theory because of his participation in the domestic violence group. He decided to use it as a way of living and apply it to his choice of behavior. During one group session, Al explained how he applied the concepts of Choice Theory to a discussion he had with his current girlfriend. He described how she was using the seven deadly habits in her attack on him for the way he was handling his ex-wife and the custody of the children. He repeated several of the remarks that his girlfriend had used and concluded by citing one particularly hurtful criticism that she had used. He realized that if his girlfriend could "hit below the belt" in the manner that she had just done, she was someone that he did not want to keep in his quality world. This was a red flag for him. He thought about it for a short while and walked away from the relationship.*

*I asked Al to use the event to illustrate the use of Choice Theory in his life. He stated that his girlfriend was not meeting his basic need of love and belonging. She was communicating with him in a manner that did not match the picture of the ideal mate in his quality world. In the real world, his girlfriend used criticizing, complaining and blaming of him in her description of what he should have done with his ex-wife. This hurt him deeply. Not only did she use it at this time, but he also realized that this was her normal communication style. His perception of her changed from the ideal mate to a person who could and would hurt him deeply. When he compared his girlfriend to his ideal mate in his quality world, he realized that this girlfriend was not a match and that his life was out of balance. His old behavior system would have had him react to the hurt with anger. After accepting Choice Theory as a way of life, he thought about an appropriate response and took the action of walking away from the relationship calmly. His total behavior was new and different from what he had chosen in the past and he was pleased with his progress and remained happy with the decision.*

*A few weeks later, his girlfriend called him and said that she had read,* Getting Together and Staying Together *by William and Carleen Glasser. The call came as a complete surprise to Al because he had not made any conditions on their separation. She knew he believed in Choice Theory and that he had read the book and chosen to live by its concepts. She said that she wanted to change and have a relationship with Al like the ones described in the book. The new information from his girlfriend led Al to decide to try the relationship again. In evaluating his total behavior and quality world, he found that he still had feelings for her and he was willing to give her another chance to be the mate in his quality world.*

# Frustration and Anger

When a client brings anger and misery into the group, it stops all therapeutic endeavors and can be contagious. If a client refuses to dissipate their anger and continues to spew it out in the group, they are asked to leave for the day or find another group. This program is for those who want to improve their lives, not for individuals who continue to use anger to force others to obey them. Frustration is an oft-occurring feeling when things do not happen to satisfy the basic needs and match the images in the quality world. The clients in domestic violence groups have let that frustration build into anger and then to rage and violence by not dealing with it as it occurs. Frustration occurs when we experience powerlessness to control our immediate environment and thus our basic power need is not satisfied. The client needs to learn the total behavior that will deal with the feeling of frustration and the basic need of power in a positive manner instead of the learned behavior that brought the courts into his real world.

The group members learn a combination of concepts. They learn that Choice Theory concepts can be used to deal with the frustration of life's situations. And, that the equality of partners in the relationship instead of the external power and control that has characterized the relationship in the past is most important.

One of the concepts discussed in the group is that the relationship is more important than either person in the relationship. If the ego of either of the partners is so great as to be supreme, then the relationship does not stand much of a chance of being successful. One way to resolve disagreements is the solving circle. After a time-out where both parties can calm down and regain cognitive control of themselves, they can then sit down and discuss the problem. If they envision a circle around them and their relationship in this circle with them, then they can both discuss what they can do to make the relationship better instead of satisfying their individual egos. Glasser states that one of the axioms of Choice Theory is:

> "*Never do anything or say anything in the relationship that experience tells you will move you further apart from your partner.*"

Alcohol consumption reduces the ability of an individual to make cognitive decisions that restrain the individual from acting out his/her feelings in situations and manners that might be otherwise considered anti-social. There is abundant documentation that illustrates this point. This documentation gives examples of people who get into situations after consuming alcohol or other drugs that place them in physical danger, social disgrace, or at odds with the people with whom they are in a relationship. For example, husbands who binge drink are three times more likely to abuse their wives than husbands who abstain (Kaufman-Kantor and Straus, 1987). Kaufman-Kantor and Straus concluded that a causal relationship between alcohol and domestic violence has not been proven because 80% of the binge drinkers did not abuse their wives. Instead, alcohol abuse may result from, or be related to; other stresses that increase the chance of violence. However, Kaufman-Kantor and Straus found that socioeconomic factors and perceived norms regarding approval of violence were associated with wife abuse, independent of alcohol use. In 60 to 75 percent of families where a woman is battered, her children are battered as well. Partner abuse survivors may use alcohol as a coping mechanism (Kaufman-Kantor and Asdigian, 1997a).

The total behaviors that will move a person further from their partner are the *"seven deadly habits."* These seven deadly habits that will get in the way of a positive relationship and bring frustration and anger into the relationship are *criticizing, blaming, complaining, nagging, threatening, punishing,* and *bribing to control.* These habits are the external control elements that push the partnership apart and can stretch the relationship to the breaking point. When I ask the clients; "Who wants to be with someone who criticizes them all the time?" The answer is always, "Not me!" The same goes with blaming, complaining, nagging, threatening, punishing, and bribing. If there are children in the union, then the client can see this much easier in the behavior of the children and the lack of response by the children to the parent's directives. Use of external control will usually drive partners and children away because no one wants to be someone else's puppet.

Choice Theory suggests that the partners can bring about a positive relationship by using the *"seven caring habits,"* i.e. *supporting, encouraging, listening, accepting, trusting, respecting,* and *negotiating the differences.* These habits bring people closer together and answer the ultimate question in the affirmative. *If I do or say (Fill in the blank), will it bring us closer together (caring habits) or will it push us further apart (deadly habits)?*

# *Terry's Story*

*Terry was also in the group for being domestically violent with his wife who is addicted to methamphetamine and alcohol. The Department of Children and Family Services investigated the home situation for the safety of the child and arranged for he and his wife to sign an agreement stating that until she entered a drug rehabilitation facility, he would move out of the house. The Family Law*

*Court gave Terry custody of his child and ordered his wife to have a monitor for her visits with the child. The Court gave Terry authority to choose the monitor and he decided to trust the parents of the wife (his in-laws) to provide safety for his child when the child visits with the mother. Terry agreed to obtain a restraining order against his wife so that she could not come near him or his home. On one Sunday visit, Terry went to pick up the child at the maternal grandparent's home. Mother was at the house in violation of the restraining order and she would not let Terry leave with the child. Mother kept blocking the path between Terry and his car. She pushed and hit Terry while he was holding the child. This put the child at risk of physical abuse. Terry decided to call 911 to have the police assist him in getting away from the grandparents' home. When the police arrived, they assessed the situation and talked with Terry, the mother and her parents. The grandparents told the police that Terry was preventing mother from leaving, that Terry was the aggressor of domestic violence and that he should be jailed for his repeat offence. The police took Terry to jail and booked him. Terry spent the night in jail and the next day Terry paid a $2000 bail bond, and was released from jail. When Terry went to court, the district attorney declined to prosecute the case because the restraining order allowed Terry to have contact with mother while they were exchanging the child.*

*Terry stated in group that before he had been introduced to Choice Theory he would have put the child down and forced mother out of the way by pushing her to the ground or hitting her. He then would have picked up his son, gotten into his car, and left.*

*Thinking about this incident, Terry decided to stop using the maternal grandparents as monitors for mother's visits with the child. He was staying at his sister's home and she agreed to monitor the visits of his wife and the child. A few weeks later, Terry called the maternal grandparents to inform them and mother that he planned to take the child camping over the weekend. If the mother wanted to visit with the child she would have to visit on Thursday evening. Mother came over to where Terry was staying without notifying anyone or obtaining permission from Terry's sister to come into her home. Mother knocked on the door and when Terry opened the door with the child in his arms, the mother was standing there, smelling of alcohol. She started yelling at Terry and threw something at him. Terry turned around to close the door and she socked him in the head as he was going back into the house. Terry thought twice about calling the police this time because of the last incident. He decided to call them the next day after things had cooled down.*

*The next day, even though Terry was hesitant, he called the police to document the incident as a violation of the restraining order. The same police officers came to his home and found a lump on his head where his wife had hit him. They took his statement and made an appointment to return the following day to take the statement from Terry's sister. On the following day, Saturday, the police took the statement of Terry's sister and decided to file felony charges of domestic violence and violation of the restraining orders against Terry's wife. While they were taking the testimony, Terry's wife was at her parent's home and she got into an altercation with her parents. Police were, again, called to the grandparent's home. The two teams of police officers communicated from home to home and the officers at Terry's residence heard the yelling and screaming of Terry's wife while she was at the grandparent's home. Terry's wife seemed to be out of control and threatened suicide. The police at the grandparent's home evaluated Terry's wife as being a danger to herself and was committed to a hospital on a 5150.*

*In class, Terry went through the Choice Theory diagram above and stated that he had changed his way of behaving because of the groups and his understanding of Choice Theory. He stated that his behavior system had changed from instant reaction with force to thinking about the ultimate desired gain and a more rational total behavior to obtain his desired outcome. He stated that the first incident had made him wary of the police when both he and his wife were there because they may have a tendency to protect the woman over the man even if the woman is the aggressor. He also realized that he could not trust the grandparents to report the truth when their daughter was in the wrong. His perceptions of the real world changed the way he viewed the events of the second incident and the changes were stored in his perceived world for future use and comparison with his quality world. Terry stated that his basic needs of freedom and love and belonging could be better met with his new perceptions of how he interacted in the real world. He replaced his old anger with the new perceptions and elevated the level of happiness in his life.*

Clients are very creative with their total behavior. They create elaborate concepts to justify their behavior and choose just as elaborate behaviors to solve their problems in meeting their basic needs. Anger and depressing are among the most common choices. Some choose drinking or drugs; some choose isolation from society; and some choose manic behavior along with the depressing behavior. Some choose listening to voices in their heads telling them what to do because they are so confused that they have given cognitive control of themselves to their inner voices.

Clients are creative in all that they do and say. Examples of creativity may be mimicking performances by actors, dancers, and athletes. There is creative acting in the things that they do. Examples of each element of total behavior are: the *action* when Michael Jordan scores a basket; the *thinking* in the solutions to problems that they face; the *feelings* in the way they attack a situation, as in the will to get ahead or win a game; and the *physiology* in the way some people have performed great feats to save someone's life. Every total behavior the clients choose has a creative component. When they choose helpful creativity and reject destructive creativity, they make more peaceful choices of total behavior. The symptoms of total behavior are created for the following three reasons:

1. The symptom helps the client to restrain the energy of anger that is always present whenever the client is frustrated.

2. The symptom is a way of crying for help, because people want to avoid an angry person.

3. The client uses symptoms to avoid situations that they fear will increase the frustration.

Many clients mask their anger and call for help by creating physical symptoms. If both clients and doctors who treat them could learn that frustration is the underlying cause of most ailments and that the client is able to create most any action, thought, feeling or physiology our brain is capable of experiencing, then they could save considerable time and effort trying to relieve the symptoms instead treating the root cause—frustration—the inability to have things go the way the client wants them to go to control others.

# Basic Needs

The quality world is the dream life that satisfies their basic generic needs. It is the personal Shangri-La, the White Picket Fence dream life, or the ideal way we picture ourselves in the world around us. Glasser describes the five basic needs as *survival, love and belonging, power, freedom,* and *fun.* We build our quality world such that it satisfies our basic needs. The quality world is the core of our lives because it motivates us to consider the total behavior that we think will satisfy our basic needs. This tight feedback loop is constantly being compared with the real world and events around us. This is the process by which we make choices on how to bring ourselves into peaceful stability. We constantly try to create a situation that will satisfy our basic needs because we cannot satisfy the needs directly.

During group sessions, I ask the client to try to establish the levels of their basic needs by looking at their past actions and desires to gain a starting reference from which to develop a description of their quality world. The clients look at others in the world to compare their need levels. They look at political leaders, successful business personalities, and sports figures for examples of power. They look at celebrities or heroes for examples of survival and fun.

They look at other life styles for examples of freedom. Moreover, they look at their relationships and the connected relationships of others for examples of love and belonging. Love and belonging is a measure of their loving and cooperating with other people. Power is a measure of their competing, achieving, and gaining importance. Freedom is a measure of mobility and desire to make choices for themselves. I explain that fun is not only playing, but it is learning as well. Most of the clients agree that the groups are fun now that they are learning something new about how to change their lives toward more peaceful decisions. At times, there is a great deal of laughter in the groups. Finally, survival is a measure not only of the desire to remain alive and healthy, but their desire to have children and be a parent. After establishing the levels of their basic needs, they look at their quality world by listing those persons, places, things, and beliefs that are important to them. This is just a starting list and as their time with the group continues, they constantly review these elements and move them around as to importance and the inter-relationship between them. They begin to see that it is often the conflict between these elements that are leading to their discomfort and can then start to get more information about them. They then make better choices to reduce the pain that leads to the frustration. These better choices lead total behaviors that satisfy the frustration. When the clients make painful or difficult-to-understand choices, it is not because they enjoy them. It is because they do not know anything else better to do. By bringing the elements out in the open for discussion of other choices, they are able to make choices that will better satisfy their basic needs.

It is my job, as the facilitator and the group, to guide the clients in a direction of actually starting to do something about their problems. This effort is the key factor in the success of reality therapy using Choice Theory. Since these clients have lived lives that are steeped in external-control thinking, the use of force to get what they want, and being controlled by others and society, the primary task is to influence them to rid themselves of external-control thinking. The clients can then realize that equality in a relationship will lead to a more peaceful relationship and the satisfaction of their basic needs.

Many clients focus on the problems of the past and the wrongs that others have done to them in the past. This focus must be turned to the present because that is the only place where the actions and thoughts can take place. Total behavior is in the here and now. The lessons the clients learn are from these past actions, but they are learned in the here and now. It is the present life situation that the client is trying to change. Most clients are court ordered and must deal with current demands on them such as attending group every week, having progress reports sent to court and/or Children's Services, other court orders. Additionally, clients must deal with people involved in the domestic violence who are not very pleased about the situation. Clients have enough to deal with in the present; therefore, to have them try to make plans at the beginning of their experience during group would not be productive. Once their lives have been stabilized, there will be plenty of time to deal with future activities. If they choose to end the relationship that existed when they were violent, then future activities might include choosing a new partner My goals are to have the clients base their new relationships on the compatibility of their new partner and as a result of what they have learned from the group and Choice Theory.

There are a number of *red flags* that represent personality differences between the client and a potential mate. The meanings of red flags are discussed in the group. The discussion starts with; "Is your relationship bad for your health or heading into dangerous territory?" I ask the clients to take this test and find out. If they answer yes to more than two of the categories, they are recommended to turn to someone for help. These red flags are suggested for people when they consider their relationship with another person because they represent difficulties in a relationship that can come from either partner.

Is s(he) someone who…

- is jealous and possessive toward you, will not let you have friends, checks up on you, and will not accept breaking up?

- tries to control you by being very bossy, giving orders, making all the decisions, does not take your opinion seriously?

- is scary? Do you worry about how this person will react to things you say or do? Does this person threaten you, use or own weapons or threaten with kitchen tools?

- is violent? Does this person have a history of fighting; losing his/her temper, bragging about mistreating or dominating others?

- pressures you for sex, is forceful or scary about sex? Attempts to manipulate or guilt-trip you by saying, "If you really loved me, you would…," or gets too serious about the relationship too fast for comfort?

- abuses drugs or alcohol and pressures you to take them?

- blames you when you are mistreated? Says you provoked it?

- has a history of bad relationships, and blames the other person for all the problems?

- believes that s(he) should be in control and powerful and that you should be passive and submissive?

- has hit, pushed, choked, restrained, kicked or physically abused you?

- makes your family and friends concerned about your safety?

One of the concepts that is taught to the clients is that by knowing the levels of your own basic needs, you can chose a more compatible partner by taking the time to get to know the levels of your new partner's basic needs. This compatibility match will minimize many of the difficulties that may arise in the future.

## *Henry's Story*

*Henry reported using Choice Theory with his 12-year-old son, Charles, after reading some of Dr. Glasser's books. Henry is separated from his wife due to domestic violence in their relationship. On one day when Henry had his children, they went to Denny's for dinner. Charles was projecting an attitude and was causing trouble for all at the restaurant. Henry told his son that if he chose to continue the attitude and disruptive behavior, he did not want Charles to come on the up-coming weekend's visit. Henry and his children went shopping and while they were walking around in the store, Charles remained distant from the rest of the group. After a while, Charles began getting closer and closer to the group and finally, Henry spoke to him and asked him if he had anything to say about his behavior. This moved Charles further away from the group. He continued his attitude for the rest of the evening until he, and his siblings were returned to their mother's home. Charles was struggling with his need for love and belonging and his need for power. The two were in conflict with each other.*

*The next day, their mother called Henry, confronted him about the situation, and tried to intercede for Charles. Henry maintained that he wanted to talk with Charles about the situation and his behavior. The mother and Henry concluded the phone call without Charles getting on the phone, but she understood that their son needed to talk with his father before he was welcome back into Henry's home. The next day Charles called and apologized for his behavior and was promptly welcomed on the next visit along with his siblings. Henry explained that he was uncomfortable being around Charles when Charles acted up the way he had done in Denny's and that their relationship was strained when Charles acted out the way he had done in the restaurant.*

Henry stated to the group that after reading the books he realized that the relationship he had with his son was more important than him using external control on Charles by punishing him for acting up in the restaurant. This was the method that Henry chose—to use the strength of the relationship to provide information to Charles about proper behavior toward others and to let him choose behavior that would strengthen the bonding between them. Henry chose to support the need for love and belonging that each of them had and the relationship between them.

A few weeks later, the children were visiting Henry again and this time they wanted to watch TV and play games on the TV. Henry had planned an outing for the family, but the children did not want to stop playing and chose not to get ready for the outing. Henry asked them several times, but then realized that his asking sounded like one of the seven deadly habits, nagging and he stopped. He retired into his bedroom to be by himself for a while and think about what would be the most effective total behavior to maintain a pleasant relationship with his children. He decided to wait until a TV program that he wanted to watch came on and then he went into the living room and switched the TV to his football game. He stated to the children that they had their time with the TV and now it was his turn.

When the children could not have their way, they then wanted to go on the family outing. It was too late and so Henry declined and continued to watch his football game. When the children complained, Henry asked if their mother let them do anything they wanted whenever they wanted. The children responded that she did and Henry answered with his expectations of the children when they were with him. Henry stated that when there was a family outing, he expected the children to consider the short time that they were with their father and that for all to have a weekend that satisfied all of their needs, they would have to consider the other members of the family in their decisions and total behavior. Henry was then starting to teach Choice Theory to his children. His children went home and told their mother what Henry had done—not letting them watch TV and then not going on the outing. Their mother informed her lawyer just how poorly Henry was treating the children. When mother's lawyer contacted Henry's lawyer and Henry's lawyer contacted Henry, Henry responded by reminding his lawyer that he was the one who had completed the parenting class and that mother had not taken any parenting classes as recommended by the Department of Children and Family Services. He also informed his lawyer that he was using a well-established psychological theory, Choice Theory, to strengthen the relationship with his children. He also stated that this was used in his domestic violence class. As the children's visit with their father continued, their relationship with their father became much stronger because they learned that they could talk about how their behavior affected the feelings of the rest of them and they could discuss their interrelationships without being told that they were wrong.

*Henry was also able to apply Choice Theory to his youngest son, Jimmy, when Jimmy started a fire in his mother's garage by playing with her lighter. Jimmy lit a cardboard box and then put the fire out by hitting the fire with a book until it went out. Henry took the children to a firehouse, the same one that his parents had taken him when he was Jimmy's age, and asked if anyone could talk with Jimmy about fires. The Captain came out and took Jimmy and Henry into his office where they talked about fires and the Captain showed them some pictures of burns. Henry's other two children were treated to a show of the fire engines and equipment while the Captain was talking with Jimmy and Henry. After the talk ended the firefighters showed Jimmy and Henry the fire engines and equipment too. This turned out to be a fun learning experience for the children. This is how Henry chose to deal with Jimmy acting out a normal interest in learning instead of punishing him for setting a fire.*

# Addictive Clients

The feeling of having more power than you previously had is at the very heart of addiction. So much so, that no mater how much power addicts may have, it is never enough. Addiction is the disease of "more." To get that feeling, there is no price that addicts are unwilling to pay. They are willing to harm themselves by staying with their addiction for the chance to gain a sense of power that goes beyond admiration and respect. The addiction even extends to their belief that they have gained so much power that people are now afraid of what they may do. Freedom also plays a part in the addiction in the sense that the addict thinks that it is his body and s(he) is free to do what they want with it. The power that no one can take their freedom away from them is the relationship between the two basic needs. What the addict seems to lack is that belief that love is what they need. They are so into power that love and belonging have taken a back seat to the thirst for more power. To be cured of their addiction, the addict must make an effort both to give and to accept enough love and belonging to satisfy themselves and to help satisfy someone else.

Two-thirds of partner abuse victims (those abused by a current or former spouse, boyfriend, or girlfriend) reported that alcohol had been a factor. For the spouse abuse victims, the offender was drinking in three out of four cases (Greenfield, 1998).

Violent incidents frequently involve alcohol use by the perpetrator, victim, or both. Alcohol use can increase the likelihood and severity of domestic violence incidents. Kaufman-Kantor and Asdigian (1997b) also found that when men experience the alcohol-related physical sensations of arousal, such as increased heart rate, they may "mis-attribute" such feelings as increased aggression or dominance. Women are less likely to make such a connection, possibly because of socialization. According to Stets and Straus (1990), men underreport perpetrating partner abuse, and female domestic violence victims tend to sustain more severe injuries than male victims.

Leonard (1992) affirmed that a husband's drinking pattern in and of itself would not be predictive of marital violence; a motivation for aggression would also be necessary. Men with a high level of negative affect, and those with high levels of hostility, were more likely to have patterns of risky drinking and to abuse their wives and children. Men with low levels of hostility were more likely to abuse their wives and to engage in risky drinking if their level of marital satisfaction is low. A high level of alcohol involvement among men who scored low in anger and depression rankings leads to the speculation that alcohol acted to release suppressed anger.

Alcohol appears to be used more frequently in violent crimes between intimates than in violent crimes between acquaintances, stranger or other relatives (U. S. Department of Justice, 1998).

Many of the clients come to group because of actions taken while under the influence of legal or illegal drugs. Addicting drugs mimic or activate the pleasure-producing brain chemistry that has evolved to inform us that one or more of our basic needs is being satisfied. Using the drugs is the client's best effort to reduce the pain of frustration in their lives. The sure pleasure effects of the drug and the total relief of the pain of their frustration takes over their mind. Treatment of the addict involves letting them see that settling for normal pleasures in life can satisfy their basic needs better than the pleasures of the drug. Life's pleasures are longer lasting, but less intense. If the client can start enjoying the normal pleasures of life then they can keep the desire for the drug-induced pleasure in check. They can maintain control of their lives instead of relinquishing it to the addiction of the drug. Many clients state that the desire for the drug induced pleasure never really goes away, but it can be controlled with less and less effort as the normal pleasures become a part of their behavioral system and quality world.

**Anger alters the mood of the individual by generating adrenalin within the body.** Adrenalin gives the person additional energy and a presence of being. Adrenalin alters the mood of the person. Therefore, adrenalin can be classified as a mood altering drug and an individual can become addicted to it just like any other drug. This fact sheds some light on the treatment of some of the aggressors.

The only effective treatment, no matter what the method of therapy, is the same with addicts as with other clients:

1.  Focus on helping all clients to learn new behaviors to recapture old relationships or gain new ones. The relationships need to be satisfying enough so that the addict no longer needs the drugs.

2.  Therapists and/or loved ones should not try to force or pressure any client to change. To use external control to try to persuade a client to change would be counterproductive because the clients are very sensitive to external control.

External control is the commonplace psychology in society. The client thinks that everyone important to him is *threatening, punishing, criticizing, blaming, complaining, nagging,* and *enabling* him to try to get him to stop using the drug.

The question that needs to be asked of the client is, *"Does drinking/using help you get closer to the people that you need in your life?"* This question places the decision on the client to make a choice based on his basic needs instead of using external control to pressure the client into not using. When others around the client use the seven caring habits, the client feels more inclined to make more choices based on his relationships and his basic needs.

AA advocates self-responsibility and honesty in the life of the addict. The 12 Steps are suggested as a way of life that embraces the tenets of Choice Theory as centered on abstinence of alcohol or the drug of choice. Alcoholics drink to get the feeling that they have escaped the control of others. One of the side effects of drinking alcohol is that the more they drink, the more they lose control over their own lives. *In a large part, the reason reality therapy with Choice Theory works is that it gives alcoholics a respite from external control without alcohol.*

Learning Choice Theory during group sessions and practicing it between groups helps the client to realize that they can meet their basic needs without the use of drugs or alcohol or the violence that often is associated with them. Glasser states, *"What happened in the past that was painful has a great deal to do with what we are today, but revisiting this painful past can contribute little or nothing to what we need to do now: improve an important, present relationship."*

# *Larry's Story*

*At one meeting, Larry related that his uncle and his grandmother were living together and his uncle got drunk and was physically threatening Larry's grandmother. Larry said that he heard his uncle yelling and threatening his grandmother in the background when his grandmother called him for help. Larry went to his grandmother's home and without confronting his uncle, Larry packed some things for his grandmother and got her in her wheelchair and took her to his home.*

*Larry and his wife were in family counseling in addition to the domestic violence group that Larry attended and he had asked his wife not to discuss the problems with anyone unless it was at the counselor's office. Larry's grandmother was staying in the baby's bedroom where they had a monitor installed. The first night that Larry's grandmother was at his home, his wife went in to the baby's bedroom, and started talking to his grandmother about their problem and the fight they had had. Larry was in the master bedroom and overheard the conversation. He became very angry and wanted to confront his wife. He had the proof and wanted to take out his anger on her. Larry was ready to really let his wife have it. When she came into the bedroom, Larry started to confront her with a great deal of anger in his voice. Larry said that at that point he envisioned the poster that is on the group wall—The Ultimate Question—and stopped his angry confrontation of his wife. He said that every time he tried to say something angry toward his wife he saw the poster and stopped. Larry said that he got so angry at me for having the poster on the wall and talking about it in group, that he quietly cursed me and the poster out for about a half an hour. The next day he had calmed down and realized that his wife probably needed to get some of the past off of her chest and talk it out with his grandmother. The next day he apologized to his wife for the one outburst he had made and that was the end of the situation. When he reported it in group, he said; "Boy was I angry with you for spoiling all of my fun. I was all ready to really get her because I had her dead to rights" and that "not only could not I yell at my wife for what she had done, but I even had to apologize to her for my angrily confronting her the day before." I just smiled and thought to myself that we must have established a caring relationship with him if he brought to mind the group's concepts in time of great frustration and anger.*

# Denial

One of the major contributors to the continuation of domestic violence in the home is the denial by all parties. Denial that the violence is happening and denial that the violence is as bad as it really is are two examples of this denial. This is a major issue in the treatment of the aggressor. Reality therapy and

Choice Theory lets the aggressor make a realistic self evaluation. With this evaluation, the aggressors can move beyond the denial into a more realistic picture of their total behavior and its effects on others. Many women think that aggression by their mate is "their lot in life" and do not expose the violence to the community. Most men who are violent in the home excuse it as being their right and deny that it is beyond reasonable arguing. The victim of the violence often has decided that they are trapped in the relationship because they cannot see any way out to live on their own. This is especially true if they do not have a profession or job skills and if they have children. The aggressive person plays on this trapped feeling by convincing their mate that they cannot take care of their family without the help of the aggressor. This is especially true for mothers with children and no marketable skills. Denial is at the center of the cycle of violence and it is what allows the circle to continue. This denial often takes the form of hope when the spouse hopes that the aggressor will change. The aggressor seldom changes without help (information) from outside sources like counseling.

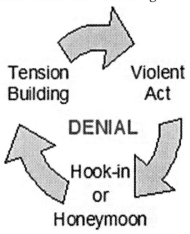

The cycle starts with the violent act of aggression, then moves to the hook-in or honeymoon phase, then to the tension building phase, and finally back again to another violent act. When a batterer starts to feel he is losing power and control, he tries to get it back in so many ways. He uses intimidation, threats, coercion. He might say he'll commit suicide, or report you to welfare if you do not drop the charges, or say he's going to DSS or immigration. He might not batter her, but he'll kick other things around, kick the dog, and put a gun or a knife on top of a table or in his pocket. He might call her names or humiliate her in front of others.

After a violent act, the aggressor has to convince the victim that the act was either a one-time thing or that he is sorry, or that the victim deserves it and that the victim cannot get along without the aggressor. The honeymoon consists of acts of asking forgiveness by bringing flowers or taking them out to dinner or giving them some sort of a gift. When hook-in is used, there is often a threat that the victim will not be able to see the children or will never have any money to live. Or there may be some other threat to the viability of the victim implying that they cannot live without the aggressor or that the price for freedom will be too high. When the victim chooses to remain with the aggressor life is smooth for a while.

Once they've filed for a restraining order, or once the guy is in jail, or once she's left, then the apologies start. They start to feel sorry for him, they think, oh, he's not able to control it and he needs me to help him. They want to fix him. A lot of times this can be the wooing stage. This is when the flowers come. This is when they say they're sorry. This is when there are dates, dinners, the I love you's, the proposals of marriage. Then the woman thinks, oh, he really loves me. The battered woman agrees to take him back, drop the restraining order, stop divorce proceedings, and take back the testimony. The batterer often tells her, and the victim believes, that they are the one person who can change him for the better.

Then the tension starts to build again and reaches an explosion point. Tensions build when the batterer begins to feel life or the relationship getting out of control. This culminates in another violent act and often it is of greater magnitude than the last. This explosive incident instills fear in the victim, and often makes that person more compliant. This can continue until the victim finally leaves the aggressor or is killed trying. Two stories illustrate how desperate the victim can become.

The first is one that I observed when I was in court on a non-related matter. I observed the victim take the witness stand while she was in a wheel chair. She had her right leg in a full leg cast from her foot to her thigh. The leg was supported straight out in front of her as she sat. Her right arm and shoulder was also in a cast so that when she had to swear to tell the truth she had to raise her left hand. Her face looked like she had been badly beaten by someone much larger than she. The eyes were black and blue and the lips were cut and swollen. She gave the following story about the events of the night in question. She stated that she had fallen down the stairs and broken her leg and arm. She stated that her husband had called 911 and then covered her with a blanket and put a pillow under her head. She told the court that her husband was very supportive of her and tried to comfort her while they waited for the ambulance to arrive. When the ambulance arrived, there were police officers too. She said that she had told them what had happened, but they arrested her husband anyway.

The district attorney then called the police officer that had made the report of domestic violence to the stand. He testified that, when he got to the home, he found the victim on the floor with a blanket over her and a pillow under her head, just as she had testified. He stated that the victim had told him that her husband had gotten angry and had thrown her against the wall and beat her up. He testified that she said that he had tossed her around the living room knocking the furniture over. The officer continued by stating that she told him that her husband had picked her up and slammed her down on the dining room table and that is how it got broken. The district attorney then asked the officer to describe the home as he had found it. The officer stated that the living room and dining room were in disarray with furniture scattered all over the place. He said that there were chairs tipped over and that a lamp was broken on the floor. He said that the dining room table was broken in half where the victim was thrown down on it. Further testimony revealed that there was a dent in the wall where she had been thrown up against the wall. When the officer finished, the district attorney asked him to describe the floor plan of the house. The officer stated that the house was a one story home and that there were no stairs in the home.

This victim was so frightened of her aggressor and/or living alone without him that she completely fabricated the story about falling down the stairs in order to cover up the domestic violence that had been going on in her home for some time. When the district attorney continued with her cross examination, the victim admitted that her husband had been aggressive toward her since they met and she countered that she loved him and that he could be sweet and loving to her. Children were not mentioned in the portion that I overheard, but if there were children who witnessed any of the violence, then they too suffer from the violence.

The second illustration comes from a time when I responded to a law enforcement call. A house had burned down and a methamphetamine lab was found in the wreckage. There were children living in the home who may have been exposed to the deadly chemicals used to manufacture the methamphetamine. When I arrived at the home, I interviewed the children and the mother. The children stated that their father had been manufacturing chemicals in the recreation room and that they had been at an aunt's home when the fire happened so they did not know anything about it. The mother stated that she had gotten into an argument with father and could see that he was very angry. She went to call 911 when she saw him walking around the living room with a five gallon can under his arm spilling something that smelled like finger nail polish on the carpet. (The firemen stated that the fire was started with acetone.) As the mother dialed 911, she felt heat on the back of her legs and when she turned around the living room went "whoosh." The mother told me that she ran out of the house using the kitchen door because the fire was blocking the front door and hallway. I concluded that if the children had been in their rooms, they would not have been able to escape and might have died as a result of the fire.

When mother went to court to testify about the events of the fire, she testified that she "might have tipped over a bottle of finger nail polish" (acetone) and it caught fire and burnt the house. By saying this, the mother was taking responsibility for the fire and trying to protect her husband from being charged with domestic violence in the home. I asked the District Attorney why the mother might have testified as she did. I was told that her husband was giving her over $1000 a week as her share of the profits from the sale of the methamphetamine manufactured in the home. The reason for the denial by mother, in this case, became very clear. She was willing to take responsibility for the fire and continue living with a man who was violent toward her for the money that he paid her.

When I related these stories to the group, they began to see just how powerful denial could be in continuing the aggression in the home. This helps them to overcome their own denial and come to grips with the violence that was in their homes. Often the aggression and violence in a client's home is less than that described above and the client is quick to point that out. The amount or level of violence in the home is less important than the fact that there was any level of violence because even a little amount of violence is unacceptable to a loving and caring relationship (using the caring habits). Having the client admit that there was violence in the home is the first step in getting them to face their difficulty in establishing and maintaining a long term loving relationship with a partner. Making an accurate self-evaluation of your behaviors is one of the major elements in reality therapy as will be shown in the example of Mike's aggression toward Judy in Part II of this book.

# 3

# Anger Management

Understanding the physiology of anger has important implications in managing anger. First, when you make yourself angry, you activate the Sympathetic Nervous System. When this system is activated certain chemicals, e.g., adrenaline and noradrenalin, are released from the adrenal glands. These chemicals pump us up and get us ready for action, whatever that action might be. Physical symptoms can include rapid heart rate, increased blood pressure, rapid shallow breathing, increased muscle tension, and sweating. Over time, other chemicals will break down the adrenaline in the body and the Parasympathetic Nervous System will intervene to calm the body down. There are actions that an individual can take while they are waiting for the Parasympathetic Nervous System to intervene. The techniques are called anger management techniques.

Anger management techniques are taught in the groups so that the aggressors can learn how to maintain their anger and compulsion to be physically aggressive under their control. These techniques begin to replace the behaviors that they learned over their many years of dealing with frustration in their homes of origin and in their neighborhoods and military careers (if they had one) or incarceration (if they served time in a prison). The clients are shown that there is always going to be frustration caused from the differences between their quality world and their perceived world. They are encouraged to change their behavioral system and total behavior so that their interaction with the real world brings about a satisfaction of their basic needs.

One of the anger management tools presented is the anger curve and how it applies to the clients' self-control of anger. The clients can modify their total behavior by learning about their physiology and recognizing the symptoms before they loose total control of themselves. The following curve illustrates this point.

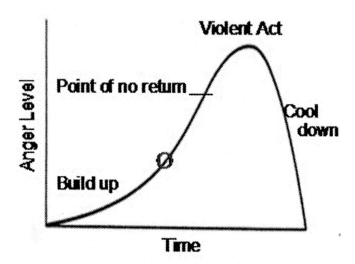

There is a period when the anger level is in the frustration range and it is building toward rage and a violent act. During this build up period we can sense our feelings and physiology and recognize that we are heading toward the point of no return as shown by the circle.

There are physical warning signs, behavioral warning signs and cognitive or emotional warning signs. The physical warning signs include increased blood pressure, increased heart rate, sweating, shaking, and dizziness. The behavioral warning signs include throwing things, hitting things or people and yelling. The cognitive or emotional warning signs include finding yourself thinking thoughts of blame against the other person or thinking that you are justified in taking the stance that you are taking.

Once we reach the point of no return, which is different for each person, we have little chance of stopping the progression toward a violent act. Cognitively practicing self awareness of our state of being modifies our behavioral system and makes this awareness more of a consistent behavior. This makes it easier for us to deal with the frustration or anger before it reaches the point of no return. This concept is related to the chart through the behavioral system and total behavior.

# The A, B, C's of Anger

**Antecedent:** Antecedents come before or trigger, but do not cause your anger. They occur at the beginning of the build up phase. This is an important distinction to remember. Anyone or anything with which you come into contact on a daily basis can serve as an antecedent for your anger. It is important to recognize and accept that you have no control over the antecedents in your life.

**Beliefs:** These are what you think about the antecedent. The beliefs come from your quality world and are applied to the perceptions that come from the antecedent. Beliefs can either be helpful or unhelpful for you, others, and your important relationships. Each of us can think differently about the same activator. You have total control over your beliefs about a particular activator and can change them when you decide that they are no longer satisfying your basic needs.

Beliefs that you choose to make an aggressive action typically include red flag words like 'should,' 'must,' and 'ought to.' To part of your beliefs, these words constitute demands made of, and commands given to, others. They are often inflexible. They are external control words and are one of the deadly habits.

You may conceal your aggression in the form of a question. For example, you are late for an important meeting and a slower car, driven by an older person, is blocking your path. You might angrily ask yourself, "Why do they let old people like that drive?" The angering belief in this case would be, "they should not let old people drive."

**Consequences:** These are the feelings, such as anger or irritation, you experience, the actions you engage in, and the physiology you create for yourself when you hold certain beliefs about the antecedent. Your actions might include throwing things, cursing, and slamming the wall with your fist. Physical consequences (physiology) might include your muscles getting tense, heart racing, blood pressure increasing and hands beginning to shake.

**Disputation:** This is a fancy way of saying that you need to argue against your beliefs. This is the most difficult part of the anger management process because you think that anger helps you control others, it's over learned and it makes you feel powerful. This is an internal self-evaluation of the predicted effectiveness of your total behavior.

**Effective Beliefs:** Once you have successfully disputed these beliefs, usually you need to replace them with effective beliefs that result in happiness. Angering beliefs are commanding and demanding in nature and include words such as should and must. Effective beliefs include words such as wishing, hoping, desiring, preferring and wanting. These beliefs recognize that you have no control over the antecedent.

**New Feelings:** Here you re-rate the original total behavior after substituting your more effective beliefs for your angering beliefs. It is this new total behavior that you demonstrate to the real world for evaluation and modification to antecedent.

Barnes Boffey (1997) introduced a way of helping self-evaluate and create a "unifying vision" of oneself. He has them ask themselves:

> *If I have the courage to be the person I wanted to be, how would I handle my present situation?*

Boffey suggests that they act as if they were that person. He has us keep the following guidelines in mind as you select your new behavior.

- Be realistic. The step you select should be simple and within your grasp; chose something you're sure you can do. We do not want any failures.

- Be unconditional. Resolve to chose this new behavior regardless of how others behave—not "only if" they do this or that.

- Be committed. Be clear that you will do this—not that you'll try or intend to do it. The level of commitment should be, at least, 4 and 5 would be best.

Once you have selected your new behavior, state what you will do differently—right away.

Another technique taught and encouraged is to practice is the time-out. The time-out is used as a method of gaining control of your physiology before it reaches the point of no return. Time-out is not used as a means of punishment or isolation from others. There are several key points to the time-out that are stressed as it is used. The first is that the method must be agreed upon by both parties. This is preferably discussed when there is calmness in the relationship and the subject can be broached without putting the mate on the defensive. One suggestion is that the client mentions it as something that was discussed in group and that he/she would like to try it so that they could come to a negotiated difference instead of having another argument. If the mate agrees to try the time-out method, it is described as follows. Either partner can ask for a time-out period not to exceed 60 minutes so that they can regain control of themselves. This way they are taking responsibility for their total behavior and not placing any responsibility on their mate. A kitchen timer is suggested as one way to keep track of the time.

If either party recognizes the early warning signs of anger described above, then a personal time-out is called for by telling the other person that you are angering yourself and you will need to leave for a period of time. Once the time-out is called, each partner stops the discussion/argument and retreats to another activity that will take their mind off of the subject. This allows them to regain their composure and return to the subject with a calmer and more objective manner. At the end of the agreed upon time, they come back together to discuss the subject. If either party starts to increase their level of anger they should ask for another time period. When both parties are calm enough to negotiate their differences, then the discussion must continue. Remember that a taking a time-out also requires you to take a "time in." Taking a time-out is one way to regain control of yourself, rather than saying and/ or doing something that hurts you or others as you would have done in the past. It is using the ultimate question and caring behaviors. Time-out is not a way to get out of settling the issue and should not be used to put the problem away until it can be brought up again at some time in the future when it can be used as a point to win another argument. Once the problem has been solved, the relationship will return to a more peaceful and satisfactory state.

Managing anger is a matter of stress reduction because stress and anxiety are major influencing factors of anger and its violent expression. Reducing stress and anxiety reduces the energy level and the likelihood of violence in the expression of anger. Some of the ways to reduce the stress that builds up by daily activities are: take a deep breath, exercise, eat well, gardening, get a massage, meditate, get enough sleep, try "guided imagery," get a pet, keep a journal, hold family meetings, talk privately with your spouse, try progressive relaxation, plan getaways, be assertive, take a day off, delegate, enlist a sympathetic ear, and set priorities and make a list.

People use assertiveness to deal with the frustration of powerlessness. The success is not in the gaining what they want, but in the asking for what they want. When assertive behavior is used, it does not demean others, but it allows one to express the frustration that is felt over a situation and requests that others assist in changing the situation to lessen the feelings of powerlessness.

The acting out of anger is the root of family violence. The understanding of the causes of the hostility is relevant to all of those who work in the field of family violence and its related studies.

There are many techniques that are discussed in the groups as part of the giving of information on the way to manage the anger in the family. These techniques are discussed in many anger management texts and lectures. One of the goals of anger management is to realize that it is not the person, the behavior or even the event that causes the person to be angry. Rather, it is how the person chooses to think (their beliefs) regarding the person, behavior or event which causes their anger. Anger has many negative natural real world consequences. Anger often leads to verbal and physical aggression and decreased problem solving. The clients are encouraged to examine their anger causing beliefs and replace them with caring habits, with assertiveness, and with increased problem solving total behavior.

One of the most important ideas to keep in mind when dealing with people who are hard to get along with is to not be controlled by them. These people often resort to control maneuvers in order to get their needs met. When you find yourself fighting all of the time, then there is a lot of mutual controlling going on between the two of you. It is up to you to stop your input to the fight or controlling behavior. You can always choose not to fight. This is a very important first step in changing your total behavior with others.

# Negotiating Differences or "Fighting Fair"

One of the caring habits is negotiating differences. Other authors have called this "fighting fair" but Choice Theory uses the term negotiating differences for this concept. How you argue, especially how you end an argument, can determine the long-term success or failure of your relationship. If you negotiate your differences, by the rules of the caring habits, an equitable settlement can be reached. A primary requirement for any fight is to maintain control of your total behavior and not that of your mate's. You do not have the license to be childish, abusive or immature. If you have legitimate feelings, you are entitled to give a reasonable voice to those feelings in a constructive way. (That includes not being self-righteous or taking yourself too seriously.) Remember that the solution of the problem is more important than winning the fight.

The basic negotiation outline should be: state your issue, suggest alternatives, and reach a solution. Do not avoid a negotiation or a question in a negotiation. State your issue as a request, not a demand or a speech. Remember that you are not a mind reader or a therapist. Let your partner state their views and listen to what they are saying instead of thinking about what you will say next.

Here are eight specific rules for fighting fair that I have modified to include the axioms of Choice Theory.

**Do not argue in front of your children.** Children learn how to behave from watching their parents and others. All we can do is give others information and we want that information to be positive instead of negative. Fighting in front of your children is nothing short of child abuse. It can and will scar them emotionally. The caring habit of negotiating differences is a positive means to settle differing views on a subject. Therefore, doing this in front of children can be a positive learning experience for the children.

**Keep to the issue at hand.** The pain that happened in the past has a great deal to do with who we are today. However, revisiting the past pain can contribute little or nothing to what we need to do now: improve an important, present relationship. (This is the 10th axiom of Choice Theory.) Do not bring up old grudges or sore points when they do not belong in a particular argument. Lay boundaries down around the subject matter so that a fight does not deteriorate into a free-for-all.

**Maintain reality.** Even though the reality is filtered through your perceptions, try to keep the discussion about the facts. Deal with what really is at issue, not with a symptom of the problem. Be honest about what is bothering you, or you will come away from the exchange even more frustrated because you will have not negotiated your differences.

**Use the caring habits.** Stay focused on the issue, instead of deteriorating to the point of attacking your partner personally. Do not let the fight degenerate into name-calling.

**Remain task-oriented.** Work toward a solution and know what you want going into the disagreement. If you do not have a goal in mind, you will not know when you've achieved it.

**Allow your partner to retreat with dignity.** Remember that this is a negotiated solution to the problem and not a win-lose battle. The manner in which the argument ends is crucial. Recognize when an olive branch is being extended to you (perhaps in the form of an apology or a joke), and give your partner a face-saving way out of the disagreement. Acceptance of your partner's point of view may be the solution to the fight.

**Be proportional in your intensity.** Most of the arguments that you have with people are not the "hill to die on" level of disagreement. Every single thing you disagree about is not an earth-shattering event or issue. You do not have to get mad every time you think you have a right to be. Getting mad is one to the deadly habits and pushes the other person away from you and a solution to your problem.

**There's a time limit.** Arguments should be temporary, so do not let them get out of hand. Do not allow the ugliness of an argument to stretch on indefinitely. The longer you fight, the more likely you are to become angry and lose control of yourself. If you have to stop fighting and take a time-out, do so and then come back and work on a mutual solution together after the time-out has expired.

The keys to living with difficult people, as stated by Dr. Primason (2004) are:

- to stay connected and try not to criticize or fight,

- do not be controlled by their behavior—set your limits, and walk away from the fight, and

- get some support by finding a friend or partner with whom you can "debrief"—tell them how hard you're working.

This book does not go into anger management techniques in additional detail because this book is intended to provide the underlying philosophy that will make those techniques useful and successful. The reader is referred to the totality of anger management books and articles currently in publication.

# Levels of Commitment

The level of commitment of the clients indicates the chance of success that the aggressor may have in actually changing their behavioral system. How hard is the client willing to work at solving their problem and gaining a better sense of control over themselves? This is the real question that relates to how successful the aggressor will be and if there will be any recidivism or a change in the aggressor's method of domination over the others in his family. Wubbolding (2000) identified five levels of commitment related to the intensity of motivation. They are:

1. "I do not want to be here."

2. "I want the outcome, but do not want to make the effort."

3. "I'll try." or "I might." or "I could." or "Maybe." or "Probably."

4. "I will do my best."

5. "I will do whatever it takes."

Level 1 represents no commitment at all and indicates that the external control from the judge has only resulted in resentment on the aggressor's part. It is like saying, "I'll sit here for the 52 weeks, but you cannot change me." I tell this level of client that all the group can do is to give you information and what you do with it is your business. This gives them permission to be stubborn and yet still be receptive to the information that is being presented in group by me and the other members of the group. They are rebelling to the external control of the system that ordered them to attend the group. I immediately give them a choice as to their behavior and let them know that I am not going to force anything upon them. This choice illustrates to them that it is their choice to learn Choice Theory and practice it in their lives. They will find out later on that they can be happier using the caring habits instead of the deadly habits but that takes time.

Level 2 represents a reluctant client. The client does not want to take any action and just wishes that he would become less angry and aggressive and that his family would leave him alone until it happens. The client who came in as a level 1 moves to a level 2 after a few weeks when they learn that others have accepted Choice Theory and that I am not forcing it upon them. They begin to accept that I really mean that they can take it or leave it. The choice is theirs. The client would like to have what the other clients are talking about in their relationships and families, but to admit it would mean that they had to admit that they were wrong in the first place. This is extremely hard for some clients to do in public even if they are doing it to themselves.

Level 3 indicates that the aggressor may be willing to take action and make a change. This level allows for excuses for failure and reoccurrence of the aggression. Commitment at this level is not very satisfying to the victim of the aggression or abuse. The aggressor may still require monitoring in visitation circumstances. The client that is at this level talks about successes in group and supports the Choice Theory concepts to the other group members. The client is willing to bring difficult situations that arise in his relationship to group for discussion, but some times argues against the use of Choice Theory concepts. They are fence sitters as to the determination of making the changes necessary to become a caring person.

Level 4 indicates a higher level of commitment and gives hope to the family and facilitator although there can still be failure and reoccurrence of the aggression. This level does not commit the aggressor to 100% success, but does restore the hope for a peaceful family in the future. A client at this level can be reported to the court as having accepted the concepts of non-violent behavior and is practicing them in his life. The judges are happy to receive these reports from the facilitator. The client will now argue in favor of Choice Theory ideas and state examples of how he was utilized them in his relationships.

Level 5 is the highest level of commitment. This is a real commitment that can be transmitted with confidence to the court and family. Such an aggressor follows through on plans without making excuses for any physical aggression. Until Choice Theory is integrated into his behavioral system and has been practiced under varying circumstances, it will not become routine in the former aggressor's life. But, the aggressor is determined to follow through with the changes needed to live by the caring habits.

Many of the clients come into the group with a low level, typically level 1 and as they progress through the 52 weeks of the group, they move through the levels. Not all of the clients move to level 5—that would be too much to expect or even hope for. The ones that do not move past level 2 are the ones that have a good chance of repeating their aggression toward their mates and/ or family. Levels 3 and 4 are progress, but still leave room for improvement and maintain a certain amount of risk to the family that aggression may occur again. Those who reach level 5 show a real commitment to live a life without aggression and moving beyond the anger and hurt of the past. Many times reaching level 5 while remaining in the previously abusive relationship requires change on the partner's and children's part. The previous victims see the change in the abuser and decide that they like the new way of behaving by the aggressor and adopt the concepts of Choice Theory for themselves. When this occurs, the entire family benefits from learning from the aggressor. It is a real pleasure to watch the clients move between the levels of commitment and know that they are going to be passing this caring way of thinking on to their families and new friends.

# 4

# Helping Children Become Adults—Parenting

Child rearing is a process that has many great rewards, but is frustrating at the same time. This chapter addresses some of the parenting concepts that use Choice Theory as their basis. This chapter is included as an introduction to these concepts and to illustrate how to deal with some of the more typical childhood total behavior with which we choose to anger. This book is not going into parenting techniques in any additional detail. Instead, the reader is referred to the totality of parenting books and articles currently in publication. The subsections of this chapter introduce discipline, alternatives to physical or emotional punishment, using the Ultimate Question with your children, and helping the child to be successful in school. Finally, this chapter concludes with the recognition of child abuse as a result of the angering in the family

Dr. Primason states in his book, *Choice Parenting* (2004): "*Parents who use choice psychology are by no means hands-off parents. They love their children and recognize their responsibility to assist in their children's development. Like a caring and careful gardener, choice parents select materials and make important choices in their own behavior. They create the proper conditions for successful growth, but go easy on control. Choice parents are unquestionably involved with their children, offering guidance and listening with interest to the children's view on whatever the latest social or practical challenges may be. The choice parent is in no way an indulgent parent. She recognizes that she must limit her own assistance and allow her children to develop their own plans and solutions.*" (Choice Parenting is an excellent book on using Choice Theory with children and is recommended reading for a more through development of the subject of parenting.)

Raising children to become adults is a multi-year full-time job. It involves discipline, caring, support outside the home, and protection within the home. Discipline is helping children develop self-control; it is not providing the external control for them. It is setting limits and discussing undesirable behavior. Discipline also is encouraging children, guiding them, helping them feel good about themselves, and teaching them how to think for themselves. Spanking is not a good form of discipline. Discipline should help children learn how to control their own behavior. Spanking is used to directly control children's behavior—it is external control. It does not teach children self-control, as good discipline should. Kids do need to know that the adult is in charge. Spanking can teach children to be afraid of the adult in charge. Good discipline teaches children to respect the adult in charge. Respect goes both ways—treat children with respect and let them have control over their own behavior—then they will respect you and listen to you. Children do as you do, not as you say. If you want your children to obey the natural rules of society, to solve their own problems, and control their anger, then you must set good examples for them to follow. Stay calm, and try to do what is fair. Sometimes your children can help you decide what is appropriate to do when a rule is broken. Do something that makes sense and will help them learn not to make the same mistake again. For example, if they write on the wall, have them help clean it up. External control in parenting believes that it is the parent's job to make sure that the child makes good choices. The Choice Theory parenting believes that it is the parent's job to help their child learn to make good choices on their on. We are trying to help our children learn to evaluate their own total behavior and make more successful, satisfying choices. Rebellion in an adolescent result from insufficient respect by the parent for the child's heightened need for freedom.

The tell-tale signs of domestic violence can be seen when some toddlers play "house." They play mommy and daddy and they hit each other, Kids model what they see. But that model can change by giving children—as young as possible—a vision of what life should be. You have to change an attitude. You have to educate people on what is the healthy way to behave and how to control their impulses. While the place to teach people how to control those angry impulses can range from the pre-school classroom to the prison cell, authorities say extra effort must be taken to reach out to youngsters before they begin to follow the violent footsteps of their parents.

There is no way to stop it this year and there is no way to stop it next year. The only way to reduce it in future years is by recognizing the problem and educating people. With study after study showing that children reared in violence are more likely to become violent adults, experts in law enforcement, education and social services insist changing behavior today will pay off tomorrow. Teaching children that everyone should be treated with respect and that violence is never acceptable is an important step. One way we can stop the cycle is by teaching kids in school that you do not need to use violence. Teaching healthy communication skills is a long range way to help. Educating boys about women, that women are equal to men, and that boys cannot use violence to get what they want is important. Those in the criminal justice, social service and education fields said thoughtful and innovative approaches must be taken to address the problem before it worsens.

Dr. William Glasser (1984) suggests that there are three ways we can relate to our children. We can do things *to* them, we can do things *for* them, and we can do things *with* them. He states that the first two are of little value. Doing things with your children will bring forth a deeper relationship between you and them and will lead to them doing things in order to keep the relationship healthy and happy. He also suggests that parenting with Choice Theory is really preventive. If it is used early on in life, the kind of discipline problems that require external control are seldom needed.

The prime consideration should be the relationship between you and your child. To preserve or improve that relationship, what you might think is best might have to be set aside if it will not cause irreversible harm to your child. Learning to respect what the other wants even though you may not agree will accomplish much more with your teen than having each disagreement escalate into a power struggle—win or loose, you always loose. The secret of a successful relationship between any two individuals when the power is not equal—parent/child or boss/employee—is for the person with the most power to do as much as he can to show respect for the weaker person's position. The use of external control with your child is probably the most deadly of habits in such a relationship. The use of the seven deadly habits will kill a relationship where as the use of the seven caring or connecting habits will nurture it. The paradox is that the more direct control the parent is willing to give up, the more indirect control the parent gains through the stronger and happier relationship with their child.

Punishment and the use of criticism, correction and coercion are the most frequent ways in which we do things to our children. We think this to provide guidance for our children. We are satisfying our power need to be effective and responsible parents. The children feel oppressed, controlled, and inhibited. To gain an equal footing, they fight back with oppositional behavior, or shut down and choose to be depressed. Which ever they do, the method is not very effective. Punishment does accomplish a few things for the parent. It may let you feel in greater control of the situation. It will teach your child to be more careful about getting caught. Your child will be less inclined to create a new solution, will feel less connected with you, and will be less interested in following your suggestions. If this is want you want for your child, then continue angering with him or her and teach them what punishment is all about.

# The Problem With Choosing Punishment Over Discipline

Some parents make the connection that it was their punishment of the child that made him or her stop the objectionable behavior. They believe that their external control of the child worked. When parents make this connection, it reinforces their tendency to use punishment because punishment seems to have worked. What really happened is that the punishment did not make the child do anything. Rather, the child decided at some point that he or she no longer wished to experience further punishment and chose to cease the behavior you found objectionable. The children remember the punishment and not the lesson that you wanted them to learn.

Punishment and the anger that produces it, is based on the myth that you can control others—including your children. You have no control over the antecedents in your life. You can only provide your children with information and then it is the child that makes the choice as what to do with that information. The only things you can control are your own thoughts and actions concerning your total behavior. Since punishment is based on the myth that we can control others, if fails to recognize that others, including children, are free to make choices concerning whether or not to continue certain behaviors. The decision to either continue or discontinue certain behaviors resides exclusively with the child. In other words, you cannot make a child do anything! The sooner that a parent accepts this fact, the happier will be the relationship between the parent and the child.

Children become resistant to excessive punishment. When this happens, the parent's need to control their child is so great that each time the child resists those efforts the parent chooses angering and external control and increases the punishment. Eventually these children, who have been punished most of their lives, no longer respond to any type of punishment. At this point, often in the teens, both children and parents are locked in an angering power struggle. The parent must stop his or her choices of punishment to stop this struggle because the child has not been taught how to deal with difficulties on his own and, therefore, cannot stop the struggle. Parents can do this by challenging their anger-producing beliefs and by reminding themselves that they cannot control their children. They can start by using the seven caring habits instead of the seven deadly habits.

The final problem with punishment stems from the fact that children often decided not to engage in certain behaviors, for which they have been punished in the past, but only as long as the threat of punishment is immediately present. Once the threat of immediate punishment is lifted, children often resume their objectionable behavior. This explains why when children reach their teens, and the freedom that goes with it, start to act out when they are away from home. They often choose drugs, alcohol or sex as ways to make a statement about their freedom from punishment. The resulting natural consequences of their choices often result in additional complications with which the parents have to deal.

So what is a parent to do?

Parents need to first discipline themselves by effectively managing their angering. Then they need to provide information for their children by letting their children experience the natural consequences of their choices. Of course, lasting physical or psychological harm to a child is out of the question as a natural consequence.

Natural consequences are those consequences that flow naturally from the choices we make. For example, if your child does not set his alarm the night before an important test, the natural consequence of that choice would be missing the test and possible flunking the test. Natural consequences are life's greatest teachers. Parental support and caring is also a part of the natural consequences so that the child knows that the parent is providing unconditional love for the child when the child makes its own choices.

The task of a parent is to guide your children by establishing a range of acceptable choices for any given situation, and then allow them to choose from within that range. The range of choices becomes greater the older the child gets, assuming that he or she has demonstrated good decision making in the past. When your children make wise choices, they get favorable results. When they make poor choices, they experience unfavorable outcomes. By interacting with them in this manner, you avoid the need to punish them and instead, teach them self-discipline; i.e., how to make good choices and behave appropriately when no one is around to threaten punishment. The strength of the relationship between you and your child is the restraining force that the child uses to make better choices.

Punishment is designed to decrease certain behaviors. Rewards are designed to increase certain behaviors. As a parent, it is important to realize that rewarding desired behavior is always more powerful than punishing undesirable behavior. Rather than looking for bad behaviors to punish, start spending more time looking for good behaviors to reward. But, rewarding to control your child is one of the seven deadly habits because the child will only do the desired behavior to get the reward and not because of a good relationship between the two of you.

We love our children and do not want to see them struggle, so we do things for them. The story of the man who was walking in the forest and saw a butterfly struggling to get out of its cocoon illustrates this point. The man went over to the butterfly and very carefully took out his knife and slit open the side of the cocoon so that the butterfly could get out easier. The beautiful butterfly flew away for about ten yards and then fell to the ground and died of exhaustion. You see, the butterfly needed to build up his strength and stamina by struggling to get out of the cocoon and when the man made it easier for the butterfly to fly away without developing fully, the butterfly could not live in the world on his own. When we do things for our children instead of letting them learn how to do things for themselves, we deprive them of the strengths they need to survive in the real world when we are not there. One change we can make as parents is to change from doing *to* and doing *for*, to doing *with* our children.

Children are much like my cats, Oscar and Cali. They will come to you when they have a need that they want to be fulfilled. They want love and belonging from you and will run from you when they want to be independent—freedom. When you give them the love and belonging that they want, they are fulfilled and can go away happy and content. It you do not give them the love and belonging that they crave when they want it, they will pester you by getting between you and the newspaper or jumping up onto your lap sharpening their claws on your legs. They will do this until you give it to them. It is this pestering that most parents choose to become upset and anger over. Most children would rather have negative attention than no attention at all. All attention feeds the love and belonging need. The reason they act out is because you pay attention to them when they are acting out and not when they are behaving. Ordering them around during these times of the child's showing of a love and belonging need destroys the relationship between parent and child—a destruction that is hard to overcome in later years.

By ordering the children to do something, the parent is doing to the child (frightening), doing for the child (thinking), and not doing with the child. Jim and his father were clients who illustrate the effect of lashing out at your child by yelling at them and ordering them to do things. Orders are great for the military, but the home needs to be a sanctuary from the external control of the real world outside of the home. The home is the one place where the parent can practice and teach the self control of Control Theory to their children and thus help them to become responsible and caring adults.

## *Jim's Story*

*I had a private client, Jim, who came in with his son, Terry, because Terry was acting out and not doing what Jim wanted. Terry was a 16 year old athlete who was exceptionally talented in soccer. He had just made the state select team for his age group and was in line for a full college scholarship with a local university. The relationship between the two was strained to the point of breaking, if not already broken. I asked Jim what total behavior that he found particularly offensive. Jim responded that Terry was not doing well in school and was using drugs. Both of these things were going to keep him from going to college. A college education was very important to Jim. Jim had his master's degree and thought that a college education was necessary for Terry to make his way in the world. I asked Terry what total behavior of his father's that he found to be particularly offensive. Terry responded that his father yelled at him. I asked if there was anything else that his father did, and he stated that the yelling was the major thing and if he would stop doing that, then he thought things might be better around the house. Terry stated that his father was very strict and wanted things done his way when he wanted them done. So, I decided to try a little experiment.*

*I asked Terry to stand up and not to sit back down until I told him to sit. Terry stood up. I then instructed Jim to tell his son to sit down. Jim looked at me in puzzlement and then asked Terry to sit down by saying, "Sit down son." to him. Terry did as I had asked and remained standing. I asked Terry if that was the way his father yelled at him and Terry responded that his father yelled louder than that when ordering him around. I then told Jim that Terry was still standing and not obeying what he had told his son to do. Jim took the challenge to see if he could control Terry more than he thought that I was controlling him. (Actually, it was Terry that was in control of the experiment and it was his choice not to sit down as his father had asked.) He told Terry to sit down with a little more force in his voice. Again, Terry said that his father yelled at him louder and remained standing. Again, I bated Jim and pointed out that Terry was still standing. Jim, speaking in a loud voice, commanded Terry to sit down. Terry held his ground and said that his father yelled even louder. By now Jim was beginning to get frustrated and angry with the whole situation and Terry was beginning to enjoy the experiment and his power that he had over his father...This time he yelled at Terry and again Terry remained standing with his arms at his side saying only one word, "louder." He seemed to be really enjoying me put his father through his paces. Finally, Jim shouted in a very harsh tone, "Sit down, NOW!" and the reaction that Terry gave was very telling. As soon as Jim had shouted at Terry, Terry covered up his face and head with his arms as though his father was going to hit him. I asked Terry if his father had ever hit him and he said that he had never been hit in the head, but he had been spanked on the bottom. This illustrated to both Jim and me that shouting at a person can have the same effect as hitting them and that Terry was trying to keep the blows of his father's voice from hitting him by covering up.*

I suggested that Jim could consider four elements in his relationship with his son and see if they improved their relationship. The four elements are: alternatives to lashing out at Terry; using the caring habits instead of the deadly habits; helping and supporting Terry in school; and helping Terry when he was hurting from the abuse that he had gotten from Jim and the external control world. Even though there had not been any physical or sexual abuse of Terry by Jim, there had been emotional abuse and neglect of Terry's emotional well-being and to a large extent the well-being of the family.

*Jim never yelled at Terry again and started to work on their relationship to satisfy their love and belonging needs that are normally satisfied in a father-son relationship. Jim was able to see the damage that he was causing to the relationship by his shouting and that it was pushing Terry away from him instead of getting Terry to do as father wanted. Jim learned that he cannot control Terry or anyone other than himself with that session and when he tried, he only drove them away from him and lessened the relationship. Jim could apply what he learned in all of the close relationships in his life, his wife, other children, friends, and co-workers because they were all afraid of Jim's loud and powerful voice.*

# 16 Alternatives To Lashing Out At Your Child

The next time everyday pressures build up to the point where you feel like lashing out—STOP! Try any of these simple alternatives. You'll feel better...and so will your child.

1. Take a deep breath...and another. Then remember you are the adult.

2. Close your eyes and imagine you're hearing what your child is about to hear.

3. Press your lips together and count to 10...or better yet, to 20.

4. Put your child in a time-out chair. (Remember the rule: one time-out minute for each year of age.)

5. Put yourself in a time-out chair. Think about why you are angry: is it your child, or is your child simply a convenient target for your anger?

6. Phone a friend.

7. If someone can watch the children, go outside and take a walk.

8. Take a hot bath or splash cold water on your face.

9. Hug a pillow.

10. Turn on some music. Maybe even sing along.

11. Pick up a pencil and write down as many helpful words as you can think of. Save the list.

12. When a child asks for your time, attention or something you can do for them, say "yes" unless there is a good reason to say "no" instead of saying "no" unless there is a good reason to say "yes." This makes the home more positive and active instead of negative and sedentary. Saying "yes" unless you can think of a good reason to say "no" takes the large gray area of "I do not really care one way or the other." and puts it into the "yes" category instead of it being in the "no" area.

13. Try to recognize the sense in your child's behavior. What is the intention behind the choice of total behavior?

14. Favor belonging over power because it will strengthen the relationship between you and your child.

15. Encourage you child to generate more effective ways of getting his needs met.

16. Convey a sense of confidence in your child's own capability to balance his needs and to make responsible choices.

These are some of the keys to parent by Choice Theory. Instead of stopping, suppressing, or controlling behavior, connect with your child through understanding and encouragement. With a strong relationship between you and your child, your child is better prepared to generate new behavior as he or she needs it. Your child can choose better ways to satisfy his needs for power, belonging, fun and freedom.

# STOP Using Words That Hurt (Deadly Habits): START Using Words That Help (Caring Habits)

*"Sticks and stones may break my bones, but words will never hurt me."*

Do you remember that childhood chant? Children use it to protect themselves against being hurt when someone is calling them names. It does not work. Words can hurt—and they do. But just as words can hurt, words also can help!

Here are some expressions that can give children confidence and raise their self-esteem:

*I love you.*
*That's great!*
*Let's talk about you.*
*I believe you can do it.*
*Believe in yourself as I believe in you.*
*You're going to be just fine.*
*You're very special.*
*Good job.*
*Yes.*

Feeling safe and loved at home is important for children. You can help them by letting them know you love and respect them. Some of the classic problems that parents have with their children are going to bed, the use of the phone, cleaning their room, and the friends that they hang around with in their free time. Choice Theory addresses these problems through the language that the parent uses with the child to discuss them. External control is the method that many parents have used in the past and they have had little or no success. A simple change to Choice Theory language can help. Examples of one possible way that parents can respond to these situations are given in *The Language of Choice Theory* by William and Carleen Glasser (1999). This book gives many more examples that are useful to parents and children. Choice Theory helps to give the people involved the self assurance to maintain dignity when they are dealing with difficult issues that occur in the life of a family. The book gives examples of the language between parent and child, love and marriage, teacher to student, and manager to employee. The following are some of the example for the parent and child dialogue.

| External Control | Choice Theory Alternative |
|---|---|
| How many times do I have to tell you? Bedtime is nine o'clock! No television tomorrow night if you do not go to bed this minute. | As long as you're quiet and do not disturb anyone, you can go to bed when you get sleepy. But before I get too sleepy, would you like me to read you a story? |
| Get off that phone right now! I'm serious. I'm just about ready to stop letting you use the phone at all after dinner. | Things with the phone just are not working out. No one can get through. Grandma said she tried for three hours last night. I'm willing to put in call-waiting, but when someone calls I need you to get right off. Can we try that? |
| Your room's a pigpen. Clean it up or no car this weekend. | Look, I'm at the point where all I want is for you to keep your door closed. But I have to be honest: I'd like you to clean up your room. It bothers me. If you want some help from me, ask and I'll be glad to pitch in. But I'm not going to clean it for you anymore. |

| External Control | Choice Theory Alternative |
|---|---|
| If I catch you anywhere near those kids again, you'll be grounded for life. All they ever do is get into trouble. | I'm frightened at the idea of you being out alone with those kids at your age. It is okay if you see them here when I'm home. If I get to know them a little better, I may change my mind. But if you have a better idea, I'll listen. As long as we keep talking, it'll be okay. |

The reader will notice that in dealing with a child, the parent needs to be willing to commit time and attention to the child. Spending time with your child is one of the most successful ways that a parent can show their child that they love and care about them. While paying attention to the child, the parent is encouraged to use the caring habits instead of the deadly habits. When your child misbehaves, let your child know you have a problem with their behavior, and then listen hard and bite your tongue.

If you can determine which of the basic needs your child is trying to satisfy with his behavior, speak to that need when connecting and communicating with them. Our total behavior is chosen to satisfy one or more of our basic needs. Then determine which of the basic needs that your child is trying to satisfy, try to help him satisfy those needs with constructive total behavior. Then you will be successful in being *with* your child in his choosing of those more constructive total behaviors.

In Chapter V in his book, *The Art of Perfect Parenting and Other Absurd Ideas*, Dr. Yellen (2004), discusses what he calls "Adultisms" and "Ego Boosters." *"Adultisms are those negative terms, phrases, or ideas that seem to be a part of parent/adult audio tapes of the mind that get replayed to the next generation simply because we once heard them. They are born out of frustration, anger and loss of control on the part of the parent. They serve no constructive purpose and only serve to undermine children's self esteem."* Adultisms are deadly habits based on the concept of external control and angering in the relationship with your child. They are stored in our behavioral system and are acted out automatically with little thought by our total behavior.

*"Ego Boosters, on the other hand make kids, and really all people, feel good about themselves and the decisions they have made. They are an important component in producing healthy, self assured, critical thinking, sensitive individuals who are not only confident in facing the challenges that await them but have the skills necessary to be successful most of the time. A few of these comments well-placed will prove fan-*

*tastic.*" Choice Theory describes Ego Boosters as caring habits and claims the same benefits as Dr. Yellen in the raising of your children. Changing our behavioral system to include these caring habits requires practice and forethought. It doesn't come over night, but does come with constant awareness and practice.

# Helping Your Child Be Successful at School

Your school-age children often spend more time with their teachers than they do with you. It is important that you, your children, and their teachers have a good working relationship. A good relationship will help your child do better in school as well as reduce stress in your life. Again, here is an example of the language of external control and the Choice Theory alternative from *The Language of Choice Theory* (1999) that will help your child be successful at school.

| External Control | Choice Theory Alternative |
|---|---|
| Do your homework now. I do not care what it is. You have to do it or no TV tonight. | Okay, I'm not going to argue with you. Let's look that homework over together to see if you understand it. And I'll be right here to help you if you get stuck. |

In his books, *The Quality School* (1998), *Choice Theory in the Classroom* (2001), and *Every Student Can Succeed* (2004), Dr. Glasser explains how schools can create quality education for students. Dr. Glasser has established six criteria for his Quality Schools. They are as quoted on page 2 of *Every Student Can Succeed*:

1.  *Relationships are based upon trust and respect, and all discipline problems, not incidents, have been eliminated.*

2.  *Total Learning Competency is stressed and an evaluation that is below competence or what is now a "B" has been eliminated. All schooling as defined by Dr. Glasser has been replaced by useful education.*

3.  *All students do some quality work each year that is significantly beyond competence. All such work receives an "A" grade or higher, such as an "A+".*

4.  *Students and staff are taught to use Choice Theory in their lives and in their work in school. Parents are encouraged to participate in study groups to become familiar with the ideas of Dr. Glasser.*

5. *Students do better on state proficiency tests and college entrance examinations. The importance of these tests is emphasized in the school.*

6. *Staff, students, parents and administrators view the school as a joyful place.*

If your child is not lucky enough to be in one of the few Glasser Quality Schools, *Every Student Can* Succeed explains how to reach and teach every student in the public schools. And, *Choice Theory in the Classroom* is a book for use by teachers who would like to experience the joy of teaching children to succeed without punishment. Reading both of these books will enhance the children's experience in the classroom.

Here are some ideas for building a relationship of trust with your children and their teachers:

- Be aware of difficulties. If you learn about a problem, investigate as soon as possible. Listen to both sides. (Many parents believe that the teacher is always right, and many parents believe that the child is always right.) Keep an open mind.

- Talk to your child about daily events at school.

- Be involved in homework. Find out if your child's teacher regularly assigns homework.

- Make sure your child has a quiet place to work. After dinner, the kitchen table can be a good place to study.

- Establish a routine at home. Set up regular times to complete homework, play, and go to bed.

If your child brings home a disappointing report card:

- Sit down with your child and look over the report card.

- Praise your child. Find at least one good thing on the report card: attendance, no tardiness.

- Be calm! Let your child tell you about his or her poor grades.

- Ask how you can help you child do better.

- Ask what your child can do to make better grades.

- Make a plan with your child's teacher and your child to do better.

# Helping Children Who Are Hurting

The first step in helping abused children is learning to recognize the symptoms of child abuse. Although child abuse is divided into four types—physical abuse, neglect, sexual abuse, and emotional maltreatment—the types are more typically found in combination than alone. A physically abused child, for example is often emotionally maltreated as well, and a sexually abused child may also be neglected. Any child at any age may experience any of the types of child abuse. Children over age five are more likely to be physically abused and to suffer moderate injury than are children under age five. The younger children, however, are more likely to be seriously injured or killed when they are abused. (Westat, Inc., 1988) Children over five are in school and will be seen by teachers and other school personnel who are mandated reporters. This provides a safety net for them. The children under five are, therefore, more vulnerable to undetected abuse.

## Recognizing Child Abuse

Experienced educators likely have seen all forms of child abuse at one time or another. They are alert to signs like these that may signal the presence of child abuse.

### *The Child:*

- Shows sudden changes in behavior or school performance;
- Has not received help for physical or medical problems brought to the parents' attention;
- Has learning problems that cannot be attributed to specific physical or psychological causes;
- Is always watchful, as though preparing for something bad to happen;
- Lacks adult supervision;
- Is overly compliant, an overachiever, or too responsible; or
- Comes to school early, stays late, and does not want to go home.

## The Parent:

- Shows little concern for the child, rarely responding to the school's requests for information, for conferences, or for home visits;

- Denies the existence of—or blames the child for—the child's problems in school or at home;

- Asks the classroom teacher to use harsh physical discipline if the child misbehaves;

- Sees the child entirely bad, worthless, or burdensome;

- Demands perfection or a level of physical or academic performance the child cannot achieve; or

- Looks primarily to the child for care, love and belonging, and satisfaction of emotional needs.

## The Parent and Child:

- Rarely touch or look at each other;

- Consider their relationship entirely negative; or

- State that they do not like each other.

None of these signs proves that child abuse is present in a family. Any of them may be found in any parent or child at one time or another. But when these signs appear repeatedly or in combination, they should cause the educator to take closer look at the situation and to consider the possibility of child abuse. That second look may reveal further signs of abuse, or signs of a particular kind of child abuse. One of the things that school personnel need to remember is the level of vocabulary of the child. The word "beat" can mean to win or to hit hard. The word "whipping" can also mean a spanking which is a legal form of physical punishment under limited conditions. So, care must be taken in reporting suspected child abuse.

## Signs of Physical Abuse

Consider the possibility of physical abuse when the child:

- Has unexplained burns, bites, bruises, broken bones, or black eyes;

- Has fading bruises or other marks noticeable after an absence from school;
- Seems frightened of the parents and protests or cries when it is time to go home from school;
- Shrinks at the approach of adults; or
- Reports injury by a parent or another adult caregiver.

Consider the possibility of physical abuse when the parent or other adult caregiver:

- Offers conflicting, unconvincing, or no explanation for the child's injury;
- Describes the child as "evil," or in some other very negative way;
- Uses harsh physical discipline with the child; or
- Has a history of abuse as a child.

## *Signs of Neglect*

Consider the possibility of neglect when the child:

- Is frequently absent from school;
- Begs or steals food or money from classmates;
- Lacks needed medical or dental care, immunizations, or glasses;
- Is consistently dirty and has severe body odor;
- Lacks sufficient clothing for the weather;
- Abuses alcohol or other drugs; or
- States there is no one at home to provide care.

Consider the possibility of neglect when the parent or other adult caregiver:

- Appears to be indifferent to the child;
- Seems apathetic or depressed;
- Behaves irrationally or in a bizarre manner; or
- Is abusing alcohol or other drugs.

## Signs of Sexual Abuse

Consider the possibility of sexual abuse when the child:

- Has difficulty walking or sitting;
- Suddenly refuses to change for gym or to participate in physical activities;
- Demonstrates bizarre, sophisticated, or unusual sexual knowledge or behavior;
- Becomes pregnant or contracts a venereal disease, particularly if under age fourteen;
- Runs away; or
- Reports sexual abuse by a parent or another adult caregiver.

Consider the possibility of sexual abuse when the parent or other adult caregiver:

- Is unduly protective of the child, severely limits the child's contact with other children, especially of the opposite sex;
- Is secretive and isolated; or
- Describes marital difficulties involving family power struggles or sexual relations.

## Signs of Emotional Maltreatment

Consider the possibility of emotional maltreatment when the child:

- Shows extremes in behavior, such as overly compliant or demanding behavior, extreme passivity or aggression;
- Is either inappropriately adult (parenting other children, for example) or inappropriately infantile (frequently rocking or head-banging, for example);
- Is delayed in physical or emotional development;
- Has attempted suicide; or
- Reports a lack of attachment to the parent.

Consider the possibility of emotional maltreatment when the parent or other adult caregiver:

- Constantly blames, belittles, or berates the child;

- Is unconcerned about the child and refuses to consider offers of help for the child's school problems; or

- Overtly rejects the child.

Although the majority of the abused children in the United States are of school age, school staffs traditionally are responsible for only about sixteen percent of cases reported each year. (NCCAN, 1992) "Teachers Confront Child Abuse: A National Survey of Teacher's Knowledge, Attitudes, and Beliefs," conducted by NCPCA, has identified a number of barriers to school reporting. These barriers include lack of sufficient knowledge on how to detect and report cases of child abuse and neglect; fear of legal ramifications for false allegations; fear of the consequences of child abuse reports; parental denial and disapproval of reports; interference in parent-child relationships and family privacy; lack of community or school support; and school board or principal disapproval. (Abrahams, etc., 1989)

In my opinion this situation can only improve with change. Teachers can become more knowledgeable about child abuse, child neglect, and the procedures followed by the child protective services. The schools and communities can support the staff that report child abuse and neglect. And school boards and administrators can become partners in preventing abuse and neglect. These will aid in reducing child abuse in the community. Since the schools see the children every day and are exposed to their emotional state of being, they are in a unique position to confront child abuse and the fear that a child has when they are being raised in an "angering home."

# II

# REALITY THERAPY
# APPLICATION

# 5

# Introduction

This part of the book illustrates the use of Choice Theory and reality therapy in a group setting for individuals who are batterers of other family members and who have a difficult time dealing with their angering total behavior as a means of combating their feeling of powerlessness in an external control world.

## Some of the Basics of Reality Therapy

Relationship is the key to Choice Theory. The relationship between each group member and me is a model for them to use in their lives outside of the group room. I try to model the following eight steps with the clients in an attempt to bring them to the point of choosing non-violent behavior and the caring habits over violent behavior and the deadly habits. By living the model in the group, they can begin to trust in a positive caring relationship. I am not always successful at being a perfect example, but the attempt is the model itself.

1. Create a friendly relationship and get involved with the client

2. Focus on current behavior of the client

3. Encourage the client to self evaluate his total behavior

4. Have the clients develop an action plan

5. Have the clients commit to action plan

6.  Refuse to accept excuses and minimization by the client

7.  Refuse to punish for not knowing or using the caring habits

8.  Refuse to give up on the client.

Some of the personal qualities of the facilitator are empathy, congruence and positive regard. The facilitator needs to be energetic in group and not give up on the clients. He/she must have the ability to see things as an advantage and not get discouraged or be a "Polly Anna" about situations. The facilitator must have a positive but not naïve view of human nature and the legal systems. He/she must have a sense of paradox and metaphors for use with the clients, the ability to communicate hope and to define a problem in solvable terms. He/she must be willing to work within the boundaries of professional guidelines, standards, and ethics and must be culturally sensitive toward the clients.

The group room has posters and diagrams on the wall illustrating the principles of Choice Theory. These are used as reminders to the client of the concepts and terminology that is being used. They are often referred to during the discussions. One of the posters on the wall lists the ten axioms of Choice Theory. Reference is being made to them regularly and they remind the clients the limitations of their influence on others. When a client attempts to bring in external control concepts and expand their or someone else's control over another, someone in the group will gently remind the client of the axiom that they have forgotten.

# Group Dynamics

The domestic violence groups have established some rules that make the discussion more free-flowing and satisfy the Probation Department's guidelines for accreditation. They start with the mandates from the Court which state that if a client misses more than 3 weekly sessions, the absences must be reported to the Court. The facility cannot determine which absences are excusable and which are not. The facility cannot allow make-up of missed sessions. The office requires the client to call before the class if he is going to be absent; else they charge him for the missed session. This places the responsibility on the client to either attend the group or call the office. The court also requires the sessions to be 110 minutes long. Since we schedule 120 minutes (2 hours) between groups, it is up to the group to establish if they get a 10 minute smoke break in the middle or end the group 10 minutes before the next one starts. Most groups elect the 10 minute break in the middle even if they do not smoke, they can go to the toilet or just talk. To eliminate confusion as to the start and stop time, my watch is taken as the master clock. This is one of the few external controls that are placed on the groups, but we have found out that there are no diversions into discussions as to when a client is late or we should take a break or end the group. Cell phones and pagers are to be turned off during the sessions.

We, the group, ask the group members to be considerate of each other and not to talk or hold side discussions while someone else is talking. We look for positive feedback from group members instead of bashing of other people or the "system." The clients are allowed their own opinions of the system without fear of being reported to the authorities, but complaints are followed by constructive ways to use the system as an aid to their satisfying their five basic needs. There are times when members of the legal community, i.e. law enforcement, judicial, and lawyers are reported to have not performed their duties as it is thought that they should. These things happen in the real world and the clients need to learn how to deal with the frustration that they cause.

I want the clients to be open and honest about their relationships and what goes on in their lives during the week, so we follow a very thin line between what they self report and what really occurred. The court mandates me to report any violation of any law or any contact with law enforcement by a person on probation. If a client tells me that he was stopped by law enforcement for speeding, then I am mandated to inform his probation officer or the court. This mandate inhibits discussion of many of the less serious violations of the law that we could discuss to determine better ways of handling. I am not a student of the law and cannot know every time a law has been broken, but I do draw a very distinct line when it comes to acting out their frustrations with their lady friends. They cannot report that they got into a physical argument with their spouse and yelled at her because, not only does it cross my line, but it is considered another violation of the domestic violence laws. If a client cannot bring up an issue without the fear of being reported, how can we deal with real life issues that are not just made up situations? I, therefore, allow them to use "what if" preceding their reports of anything that might be reportable to the court as a violation of probation. In this manner a client can bring to the discussion situations that are more realistic and the group can help them learn how to deal with them in the future without resorting to elevating the level of anger. Real life situations are more constructive in the learning process than ones that are made up by a group member or me.

Finally, we allow and invite those group members who complete the court mandated sessions to return, free of charge, to discuss any issues that may arise after they graduate. Group members take us up on this offer and bring many practical experiences to be discussed in the group. They have commented that it helps them deal with problems of a personal nature and provides a safe place to discuss those problems with the group and facilitator in order to gain resolution and happiness.

The key to changing the pattern of aggressive conduct is self-evaluation and awareness. As with any important behavioral change, it occurs only when the person exhibiting the behavior becomes impressed that it is essentially self-defeating and resolves to try a new behavior. Aggressive people are typically not very reflective and often seem sensitive to self-examination. They find it too challenging and even painful to consider that they are perpetuating their own problems and difficulties. Punishment, external control, is not a very effective method to increase the aggressor's self-awareness. Instead, punishment encourages more anger and aggressive behavior. With the tools of Choice Theory they can find better ways to satisfy their basic needs through non-aggressive total behavior.

Group therapy as described in Wubbolding (2000) *Reality Therapy for the 21st Century* has four stages, initial, transitional, working and termination. In the initial stage the facilitator addresses the need for belonging so that everyone feels included in the group. Each client is asked what they want out of the group, what is their life direction, specific actions, ineffective and effective self-talk, feelings, and even physiological behaviors. Since the domestic violence groups are revolving groups and a new one does not start each week or when a new member comes to the agency, the need for belonging is addressed for each new member on their first meeting in the group. The new member is told the rules and guidelines, which readdresses them for the older members, and the new member is asked to describe the event for which he was arrested and sentenced to the group. In this way, he tells his personal story. Many times he minimizes his behavior or denies doing anything wrong, but this is addressed by going over the definitions of domestic violence and showing him how he is included in the definition. Minimal acceptance by the client is a start to addressing his aggressive tendency to try to control others.

The transitional stage described by Wubbolding (2000) addresses the power need of the client when anxiety, conflict, and resistance to the concepts arise. The facilitator uses his skills of the caring habits, supporting, encouraging, listening, accepting, trusting, respecting, and negotiating the differences, to develop a caring relationship with the client. Again, since the group is a revolving group, this is done throughout the entire time that the client is in the group. As the group members become stronger in their commitment to Choice Theory and non-violent or non-aggressive behavior, they support the newer members of the group by use of the caring habits too. This is pointed out by the facilitator as evidence of member maturity.

In the third stage, the working stage, love and belonging is addressed. Wubbolding (2000) addresses this "when the group members come to believe that others in the group can be of some help to them." Wubbolding states, "The central importance of this phase is illustrated by the emphasis given by the therapist to helping group members evaluate the various aspects of their own control systems: wants levels of commitment, and total behavior." He continues, "At this stage therapists ask group members to assist each other in making self-evaluations." In the revolving group, this occurs at each meeting. The people who have been in the group longer confront the statements and behavior of the other members that do not seem to be consistent with the caring habits. It is this confrontation that the facilitator must monitor to maintain a caring community for the less experienced members. Monitoring of each member's activity during the past week brings up topics that need to be addressed for the group. There are groups when the current topic of a member takes the entire group time and all members are encouraged to participate in the discussion with their ideas, suggestions, and opinions. The entire discussion is summarized as the 7$^{th}$ axiom of Choice Theory given below which states; all we can give or get from other people is information. How we deal with that information is our or their choice. One of the major differences between reality therapy and Choice Theory and other therapeutic interventions is that the facilitator is not telling or directing the clients how to behave. The facilitator gives information and asks the client to consider it to see if the information will better satisfy his basic needs. If the client accepts the information, then he asks to establish a plan to implement his use of the information. Progress on the plan is then monitored on a weekly basis.

Wubbolding's (2000) final stage is the termination stage. In it he states that further planning helps address the fun and belonging needs in addition to touching on the freedom or autonomy needs. The revolving group addresses these needs throughout the normal sessions when a member is coming to the end of his court order time in the group. Most of the group members have experienced a loss of freedom when they went to jail for their crime. Additionally, for the duration of the time in group and doing their community service, their free time and money has been taken from them. One of the questions that are addressed during the sessions is: Was your behavior worth the price you had to pay in freedom of time and money?" The answer is always "NO!" Many clients state that what they learned from the groups was worth the time and money spent, but they wish that they could have done it without all of the court intervention. They do admit that they would not have taken the class if it was not mandated by an external control force.

# External Control vs. Choice Theory

External control is used by most of the civilized world in an attempt to maintain an orderly society. The key word is "orderly" and it is defined by those in control of the rest of the people. External control is externally motivated and realities are the same for everyone. It is based on the premise that those in power can control others, that events control me instead of me controlling events, that coercion is best to get others to follow the rules, and that it is a win/loose proposition for all. External control leads to the feeling of powerlessness that leads to frustration and then to anger, hostility and ultimately violence. When someone in our world is not providing satisfying total behavior, the control imperative suggests that we try harder to change them. They do not like it, and they tend to push back. The harder we try, the harder they push back until the relationship is broken and the people distance themselves from one another.

The violence is used in an attempt to get others to do what the aggressor wants them to do. Violence is used throughout the world in an attempt to control others. It is like saying, "I know what is best for you and I'll force you to do things my way so that I can be happy because you cannot be happy unless I am happy." I ask the members of the group when they first join the group if they like the judge controlling them and making them take this group. I have yet to get an affirmative answer. Then I ask them, "Why do you think that anyone else likes for you to control them?" Then I tell them that we will provide them with some information and let them make up their minds what they want to do with it.

Experts say jailing abusers will not stop the violence—or solve the domestic violence problem in the community. They note that, without treatment, abusers will continue the cycle of violence and probably wind up back behind bars. The external control proponents believe that success in most of the batterer's programs stems from the batterer's fear that something—his wife, family, home—will be taken away. It is those people who do not care about what they might lose who are the most difficult to treat. Choice Theory proponents believe that Choice Theory can be taught to all aggressive people with success.

Choice Theory as differentiated from external control teaches the following:

- that we are internally motivated,
- that our realities are different from each other,
- that we can only control our self,
- that events just happen and we have choices on how to react to them,
- that we maintain an orderly relationship with collaboration, and
- that it is a win/win proposition for all people.

Choice Theory places the responsibility of orderly conduct on the individual and the therapy teaches him how to make decisions that will meet his basic needs without infringing on the basic needs and happiness of others. Choice Theory leads to self reliance, internal power and control, choice of ones' actions and ultimately happiness and internal peace.

The language of Choice Theory is used in the groups. It is important because it reframes the thoughts of external control and of powerlessness into that of inner control and Choice Theory. Some examples of the change in language are given below:

| External Control | Choice Theory |
|---|---|
| I cannot. | I choose not to. Or I will not. |
| He made me do it. | I chose to do it. |
| You do not give me any choice. | I do not see that I do not have any choices. |
| My parents will not let me… | I choose to do what my parents want. |

| External Control | Choice Theory |
|---|---|
| I cannot stand it. | I chose not to tolerate it and left the area. |
| A fit of depression came over me. | I chose to depress. |
| I had an anxiety attack. | I chose to be anxious. |
| He makes me sick. | I choose to be sick when I am around him. |
| This rain gets me down. | I choose to depress when we have rain. |
| She really gets to me. | I choose to get upset regarding her actions. |
| My job is stressful. | I choose to react with stress over my job. |
| That situation upsets me. | I choose to get upset over this situation. |
| My child is such a worry to me. | I choose to worry over my child's behavior. |
| You did not tell me. | I did not know. |
| That kid drives me up the wall. | I get upset with this child's behavior. |

Just reading the Choice Theory statements, the reader should feel better about the way things are stated. The statements tend to give one a sense of empowerment and self control.

# Domestic Violence Defined

Let me first give some of the guidelines that law enforcement uses in determining if domestic violence has occurred and who is the aggressor. The *domi-*

*nant aggressor* is the *most significant*, not necessarily the first, aggression. The officer shall consider:

- Intent of the law to protect domestic violence victims

- Threats creating fear of domestic violence

- History of domestic violence between the two

- If either acted in self-defense

- Presence of fear

- Credibility

- Offensive/defensive injuries

- Seriousness of injuries

- Corroborating evidence

- Height of parties

- Weight of parties

- Use of drugs/alcohol

- Amount of detail in statement

- Level of violence

- Criminal history

- Existing court orders (past and/or present)

Domestic violence is considered a felony if there is injury to one of the parties. If the law enforcement officer did not witness the violence he/she can make an arrest for an assault based on probable cause. This is based upon locating and evaluating evidence such as statements of the parties, statements of witnesses, behavior of the parties, physical evidence at the scene, and injuries to the parties.

Battery as defined by a judge when I served on a jury is "touching a person, their clothing, or immediate possessions while you are angry." The definition does not include a description of any injury—just "touching."

The judicial branch uses the domestic violence groups in cases that involve anger management or where the bench believes that anger management counseling would be of benefit to the client(s).

The above information is discussed when the client comes to the group so that he may get an understanding of why the court mandated him to attend a group. This discussion usually reduces the resentment of the client for being court ordered to the group. It also allows the client to accept the ruling by being included in the just "touching" category. Most clients will admit to touching their mates while they were angry even though they claim their mates hit them also.

# 6

# Using Mike's Story to Illustrate Group Reality Therapy

I will use a particular situation of one of the group members to illustrate the interaction between the client(s) and the facilitator. Mike's story provides the framework for this example. Mike's counseling occurs in a group setting with up to 15 clients in the session. Most of the clients are court ordered to be in group for 52 weeks and come to the group with resentment about the external control that sent them to the group. When Mike first came to the group, he minimized, and even denied the violence of his behavior and the stressful events that led to making him use violence against his domestic partner. It is very difficult for a man to talk in front of a group of strangers and tell them what he did in beating up a woman. Mike knew that he had done something for which he was ashamed and he could not brag about hitting a woman or frightening her so much that she did not want him around her or their child. A significant number of clients were under the influence of drugs or alcohol when they committed the crime, but Mike was not using at the time of the incident. Those clients who were under the influence, often state that they cannot remember what happened as a way of not facing the reality of their actions.

Mike is a big man, 6 ft., 275 lbs, shaved head, and a few tattoos on his arms. He has already completed one court ordered domestic violence program that was based on an external control model and attacked the men and their way of thinking without giving them positive reinforcement and goals. He was separated from Judy, who is his girlfriend and the mother of his child who was three years old, because of his acting out in threatening manners around his child and Judy. They separated with the understanding that it is a trial separation to get back together without living together. Mike was married previously and when that marriage dissolved due to his violent behavior, he lost custody of his child by that woman. His ex-wife has obtained permission from the court to allow her to move away from Mike. The court also ordered Mike to have monitored visits with the child. Mike is unable to visit very often because there is no one in the town where she lives who will monitor his visits; therefore, he must bring someone from Los Angeles with him who is acceptable to his ex-wife to monitor the visits. Since his ex-wife lives about 300 miles away from Los Angeles, it is virtually impossible for Mike to arrange a visit.

One day Mike went to Judy's apartment and found another man with Judy. This man's psychotropic medicine was on the table where his daughter could get to it. The apartment was on the second floor and the front door was the only normal entrance or exit. Mike looked at the apartment through the window and judged that the apartment was dirty and messy and this was a threat to his daughter's health and safety. (The condition of the apartment had been one of the issues that he and Judy had fought about and which led to her asking him to move out.) Mike entered the apartment using his key. Judy and the man took one look at Mike and retreated to her bedroom and locked the door. Mike kicked the bedroom door open and entered the room. The man was frightened by Mike's appearance and jumped out of the bedroom balcony to get away from Mike. Mike told Judy that he was only going to "talk" with the man, but his facial expression and body language indicated that he was extremely angry. Judy was frightened and called the police. Mike was arrested and charged with vandalism due to the broken door. He was not charged with domestic violence because he did not strike anyone or make any threats to harm anyone. Mike was ordered to take 52 more weeks of Domestic Violence counseling for his actions because the court saw the incident as an act of violence and since Mike had already taken one domestic violence group.

# Basic Needs

For this model, the brain will be considered to consist of two parts, the cerebral cortex and the part which is considered the reptilian brain. The cerebral cortex contains all conscious and voluntary need satisfying behavior and the reptilian part of the brain is used for automatically monitoring the basic needs of survival. Psychological needs arise in the cerebral cortex.

The fundamentals of human motivation are derived from five basic needs—*survival, love and belonging, power, freedom* and *fun.* Like intelligence, these needs are genetic. The choices we make are the ways that we satisfy them. These needs do not change throughout a person's life, but the manner in which each need is met or addressed does change. Health and happiness come from meeting the basic needs through involvement with others. Each of us has a strength level for each need. The total population has a distribution similar to that of our intelligence quotient—a standard normal curve. A similarity in the strength of each and all of the needs is important for a lasting relationship. If we take a standard deviation of one rating point, then it is suggested by Dr. and Carleen Glasser in Getting Together and Staying Together (2000), that a relationship will have difficulties in the need area if there is difference greater than one rating point in the need category. The clients are encouraged to determine the strength of their own needs to form a basis of establishing a stable relationship with a partner and to understand themselves, their needs and their wants.

If we use a scale from one (1) to five (5), then on the Normal Curve below, three (3) would be average and 68% of the population would fall between two (2) and four (4), and 96% of the population would fall on the scale from one (1) and five (5). 2% would fall below the level of one (1⁻) and 2% would fall above the level of five (5⁺). The nearer that your need level falls to average level of three (3), the more people will fall within +/-1. The closer you are to the ends of the curve, one (1) or five (5), the lesser number of people will be compatible to you.

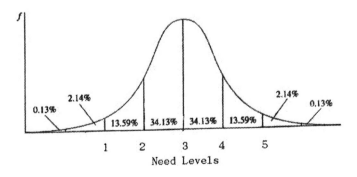

The needs are:

- Survival

- Love and Belonging

- Freedom

- Fun

- Power

The first of these needs is a biological need that we share with all living creatures that strive to maintain physical well-being and reproduce. The others are the uniquely human psychological needs. We differ from one another in the relative strength of our needs, but we all have the same ones. We cannot change or control our basic needs that motivate us, but we can control our choice of specific behaviors to satisfy those needs. We always choose total behavior which we hope will satisfy one or more of our basic needs.

Back to Mike and Judy; I asked Mike to look at the basic needs and to review them for possible application to his situation. He took several minutes and then stated that he was ready to go ahead. Mike had to determine his need levels so that he could determine the importance of each need to himself and his happiness. We will look at the level of Mike's needs as we look at things that are in each need category.

## Survival

The need for survival and physical well-being drives our healthy behavior. The elements of survival are food, shelter, safety, and reproduction. Reproduction is included as an element of survival because it is the basic element in the survival of the species and this is an extremely strong drive in our lives. The strength of this drive may vary with age and sex, but it is always a part of our reptilian brain.

Mike determined that he had a survival need level of about $2^+$ on the scale. Since he had been in the Marines he had learned to take care of himself and could count on his training to keep himself safe in most situations. He was a skilled construction worker and believed that he could always be able to support himself and his family. His children were important to him and they were a key element in his decision to be close to average in survival.

The primary survival need that was not being met in Mike's case was the survival of the species. Mike stated that he has always been protective of his daughter. This is not uncommon with the men of my groups. He felt powerless to control the safety of his daughter while he was out of a loving relationship with her. Mike viewed the other man as a threat to his child and judged Judy as putting his child in a dangerous situation. He thought that the drugs being left out on the table where his daughter could get to them were a hazard and that he wanted to keep his daughter safe from such hazards.

# Love and Belonging

The need for love and belonging drives our social behavior. It feels good to us to be connected with others, to be understood and to thought of by others. The elements of love and belonging are friendship, caring, and involvement. When a person is a toddler, the love and belonging need is primarily met by family and a few close family friends. In the teens, a person relies more on their own friends and when they get married and go out on their own, they have their mate and their own family to primarily meet this need.

Mike perceived that his relationship with Judy was bad and not satisfying his needs. He thought that he had a need level of 4 because he wanted to have people in his life that he loved. He had not been meeting this need because he had been pushing his loved ones away with his anger. Mike had been married before and his total behavior of angering and raging had made him undesirable to his wife. They had divorced and she had custody of his son. Instead of changing, Mike just went out and created another family with Judy. Mike perceived that Judy was preventing him from a good relationship with his daughter. Mike was blaming Judy for this distancing just as he blamed his ex-wife for his not being able to have a relationship with his son.

Blaming others for their problems is typical of people who have not learned Choice Theory or to take responsibility for their actions. They think that since they can control others that others can control them too and the world is an external control world. They do not understand that being "attractive" is more successful in a relationship than being controlling. Mike's total behavior was making him less attractive to Judy and his daughter and actually frightened them away from him. He would have to change his behavioral system and total behavior before he could attract Judy and his daughter back into his life.

# Power

The need for power, achievement and self-worth drives our productive behavior. Positive self-worth is tied to the basic need for power and is derived from accomplishing quality work. When we are effective, we feel proud and worthwhile; when we are not successful, we feel frustrated and our self-worth suffers. The elements of power are competence, achievement, recognition, importance, skill, and respect.

Many, but not all, of the group members are laborers or unemployed with, at most, a high school diploma. Their self esteem is low and they do not think that they are highly respected in the community. They often come to group saying that their partner "disrespected" them and that is why they tried to force her to respect them. By "disrespected" they mean that the person did not ask for permission to do or say something (as though they had the authority over that person to give permission). Reaching a point in your life where you feel that you are competent at something and have achieved a certain level of recognition and importance is an internal concept. The competence comes from within oneself and not by recognition from the community. There are many who have gained community recognition without feeling the elements of power in their lives. These people continue to strive for more and more power and control over others.

Often there is a delicate balance between power and love and belonging because, unless treated properly, the two are at cross purposes with each other. Power can be an individual goal and require individual control over the surrounding environment and people, where as, love and belonging is a mutual commitment and often requires give and take and equality of importance between individuals. Those families who have members in powerful positions have to be very careful of their family commitments to maintain the love and belonging balance in their relationships.

Mike stated that he felt powerless to control the situation, so he used his physical power in an attempt to satisfy his power need. He thought that his power need was at a level of 3+ but conceded that it may be more important than this love and belonging need, which he had stated to be a level 4. This shows the difficulty he had in trying to separate these two needs and arrive at an evaluation of each, independent of the other. After a discussion of the issue, he still thought that his power need was less than his love and belonging need. Since there is no absolute test for the level of these needs, these levels are still self-report statistics.

The more he tried to hold on to his relationship with Judy and his daughter, the more they slipped away from him. It is like trying to hold onto a handful of dry sand—the harder you squeeze, the more sand you lose. Mike wanted to control the situation and force his solution on the others so he exerted external control over Judy and the other man. His solution was basic. He wanted Judy to be a stay-at-home wife. In that manner Mike could satisfy his need for power and control over Judy and his daughter. Mike was replaying a scenario that resulted in trouble with his ex-wife and son.

# Freedom

The need for freedom drives us to be independent and to choose our own course. When we try to determine that behavior and choices of others, they do not like it. It inhibits their basic need for freedom. The elements of freedom are choice, autonomy, independence, and liberty. Freedom is a coveted concept. Being able to choose what satisfies our needs instead of being subjected to the choices that satisfy others' needs is the basis for happiness. There is a delicate balance between freedom and love and belonging because it demands opposite characteristics in a relationship. Autonomy and independence imply that others are not consulted in the decision making process. Love and belonging, on the other hand, implies that others are taken into consideration when making a decision because it is a decision that affects those who are close to you. With freedom, others are considered, but just not consulted as to their wishes and desires. When we try to determine the total behavior and choices of others, they do not like it and shy away from us. It inhibits their basic need for freedom. Therein lays the major cause of conflict in all relationships.

Mike did not consider his need for freedom when he chose to act out his perceptions with total behavior that included threatening acts. He stated that his freedom need was below average and thought it to be about 2 or $2^+$. Mike's love and belonging need was definitely higher than his freedom need because he placed his need for his daughter and Judy above his need to be without them. But, he admitted that he was thinking only of himself and not in the long term either when he entered the apartment.

Mike did not consider the possibility that the legal system might take away his freedom for a period of time by putting him in jail. He did not consider that he might be on probation for up to three years. This means that the court would have control over him for that period of time. He also did not consider that Judy would choose not to want to be around him or have their daughter around him because of his angering. Thinking is a component of total behavior. Mike did not think of the consequences of his actions prior to his acting out with a violent action.

# Fun

The need for fun drives our search for discovery and our interest in play. The elements of fun are pleasure, enjoyment, liberty, and learning. You will notice that liberty is both a part of Freedom and Fun. Liberty brings fun into a life as opposed to constraint, which brings tension and frustration into life. Fun includes going to Disneyland or the park for a family picnic. Fun is enjoying what you are doing. Learning can also be considered as fun. Remember when you were five or six years old and you learned a new song or joke or how to play with a yo-yo? It was fun and you wanted to share that fun with those around you, especially your family and close friends. Love and belonging, too, is a part of the fun need and that is why it is stated that love and belonging is the key element in happiness.

Mike was unable to connect with any of his fun needs that were affected by the incident. He thought that his fun need was about average, a 3 on the scale. He did admit that being in the group was a learning experience and that he enjoyed coming to the sessions each week. It provided a place for him to "get his head on straight" and discuss his week's events. He also enjoyed helping other clients with their issues. After a discussion, Mike decided that he had sacrificed some of his fun needs by being in jail and controlled by the judge.

He did not see any fun in what *happened* in the incident that brought him to the group. This indicates that his chosen total behavior did not satisfy all of his needs. He did not choose a total behavior that addressed his fun need. This is typical of abusive aggressive behavior. There is often little or no fun in it for you or those you hold close to you. Aggressive acts encompass most, if not all, of the deadly habits—*threatening, punishing, criticizing, blaming, complaining, nagging,* and *enabling.* Aggressive acts push people away instead of bringing them closer to us and aggression violates the ultimate question. They are not fun.

The overall rating of Mike in the needs is Survival ($2^+$), Love and Belonging (4), Power ($3^+$), Freedom (2 or $2^+$), and Fun (3) which describes a fairly average person.

# Quality World

Our quality world is the source of all important behavior. It contains what we want most. As we live, we build a special place in our memory that is filled with specific ways to satisfy one or more of our basic needs. The quality world is the most important part of our lives. We feel very good when the elements in our quality world are satisfied. It feels very bad and we are frustrated when the elements are not satisfied. Our quality world consists of people, situations, and beliefs which satisfy our five basic needs. The quality world is personal, not external or worldly. No two individuals' quality world is the same.

For a couple to have a long-time, loving relationship, William and Carleen Glasser (2000) state that their quality worlds must be similar. Most likely they will differ only in the intensity of quality of the elements within the world. We pay attention and will work hard for what is in our quality world and do not care much for what is not closely related to elements within our quality world. The elements in our quality world usually take the form of pictures, ideas, or concepts that we believe will satisfy one or more of our needs. We store the memory of experiences that, at the time of occurrence, felt good and satisfied one or more of our generic needs.

Our quality world is built from the way we picture and perceive three very common but different kinds of life experiences—interactions with important people; interactions with things; and systems of belief that drive the total behavior from the behavioral system. The pictures in our quality world are very important and difficult to change because they were built on good feelings. Our choices are governed by our wanting to feel as good as we can now and in the future. We hold pictures of people, things, and beliefs that we have enjoyed in the past, or are enjoying now, or hope to enjoy in the future in our quality world. These pictures stay in our quality world until replaced by something that brings us more joy. The main criteria for keeping a picture in our quality world is how good the feeling or experience was when we chose to put it in. This is one of the reasons that people stay in intimate relationships—the initial love relationship is such a good experience that it is very difficult to remove it and the person from our quality world. We spend our time desperately trying to recapture the pleasure we had when we courted each other. This initial love relationship often masks the violence in an angering home and sets the victim up to remain in the relationship and continue being abused.

For example, Mike had friends in his quality world that Judy did not even know. I, for one, was such a person. Judy knew about me and my relationship with Mike, but she had never met me or communicated with me in any manner. There are elements in our quality world that are not secret from our loved ones, but are still held to be very important. This just states that, even for those closest to us, we do not know how important the elements in their quality world are to them. Respecting these unknown parts of our loved ones places the relationship above our self interest. In other words, the relationship is greater than each of us in the relationship.

Mike had Judy and his daughter in his quality world. Mike also had his son by his ex-wife in his quality world even though he was not able to visit him as often as he would have liked. Mike also had the belief that he could overpower others to get them to do as he wished. He had been able to use force in his life to get what he wanted and so he believed that if he wanted something, it must be right for him to have it. If Mike ruled the world he would have everybody do as he wanted and be the way he wanted them to be.

Mike also believed that it was wrong to "snitch" on Judy in order to have the authorities intervene. He could simply tell Judy how to run her life. He knew that he could not control the authorities and did not trust them to do things as he would do them. He could tell Judy how to take care of their daughter and she should do as he said. He did not consider her need for freedom. He had little or no empathy for Judy or for his daughter either. He could not put himself in Judy's shoes and accept her for who she was and what she had in her quality world. Remember, a home that looked like a barracks was not in Judy's quality world. Judy's quality world was not a home that resembled a barracks.

# Perceptual System

The perception system consists of the physical sensory system, the total knowledge that we have accumulated over the years of our lives, and the values we place on what we perceive. It is how we perceive the real world. The only way we know the real world exists is through our ability to perceive it through our senses. All of our senses make up the sensory system.

## Sensory System

This system includes the touch, sight, hearing, smells, and tastes. We develop likes and dislikes on each of the things that we sense. We relate to the real world by use of our sensory system. Everything that we sense is evaluated by our senses as it is transferred from the real world into our perceived world. For example, if you wear glasses, as I do, then the lenses alter the real world image in such a manner as to correct for the distortion in our sight system. The smells that we bring in through our noses are compared with the learning of smells that we experienced when we were children. The smell of mother's apple pie cooling in the kitchen or chicken frying in the pan is an example of these smells. The principle applies to our sense of taste. Our hearing sensitivity is subject to any birth defects or abuse we may have encountered in our life. Our touch sensitivity and detection system is honed to a fine point by use and observation of the items that we encounter. We start developing our knowledge of senses when we are born and continue through out our lives.

## Total Knowledge Filter

Our total knowledge filter contains all of the facts and concepts, understood or experienced. It does not place any value, positive or negative, on the knowledge. This filter separates the perceptions into three categories—rejection as meaningless, accept conditionally until we can find out if it is meaningful or not, and accept absolutely because it is meaningful to us. The total knowledge filter rejects those things that we know to be unimportant or irrelevant to our current situation. We totally disregard those elements of the real world that we deem to be irrelevant and not connected with the thoughts and ideas. The filter lets those things, that we think might be pertinent to the subject we are addressing and concerned with at the present time, pass to the valuing filter. The perceptions that are passed thought the total knowledge filter are then evaluated by the valuing filter.

## Valuing Filter

The valuing filter is the filter we use to place value on those elements and thoughts that pass through our sensory system and total knowledge filter. These are the elements that are meaningful or the ones we want to find out about. We compare each element of the current situation with our values and quality world pictures and then place a level of pain or joy to each. This level can go from very painful for unsatisfying feelings or negative values, through neutral values when we have no feelings about an element, to very pleasurable for satisfying feelings or positive values. We tend to put a negative value or pain on what we perceive is opposed to anything we want. We tend to put a positive value or pleasure on what we perceive matches our quality world. We tend to put a neutral value on what we perceive is neither opposed to, nor particularly close to anything we want.

Mike perceived the external control of the judge as unfair, and thought that his actions were justified. Mike kept saying, "I only wanted to talk with the man." Mike did not think about how he looked to Judy or the other man. Our actions communicate twice as much information as the words that we speak.

He perceived the pills on the table as a threat to the safety of his daughter. He perceived the messy home as "dirty" and not as a fit place to raise a child. He perceived Judy as the person who was responsible for all of this danger to his daughter. He perceived the other man as the threat to his continued life with Judy and his daughter. Mike had a prior marriage and another child. The prior wife would not let him see that child after their separation. He perceived that there was no one who could help him so he needed to take matters into his own hands.

# Perceived World

Our perceived world consists of our perceptions along with the values we placed on them. It contains many more pictures and concepts than our quality world. It contains the total history of the perceptions that we have gained during our life. Our perceived world represents our total knowledge or what we can remember. We take this world and compare it with our quality world. It is from our perceived world that we generate the frustrations from painful feelings, the pleasures from happy feelings, and the acceptance from those feelings that do not have a bearing on the present situation. This is the way we see the world. It is very dependent upon our historical upbringing, current self esteem, and the self worth that we feel about ourselves and our ability to deal with the situation at hand. No two perceived worlds are the same because each of us has different experiences. What we perceive as reality or the real world is, therefore, not real or objective. The reason that we can get along with each other is because many of us perceive the world in similar ways or essentially the same.

Realities, objectivity, sanity, truth, right, wrong, good and bad are a few examples of what we believe as real. The reality of aggression in an argument is also a matter of perception. If the more aggressive person believes that he/she was too aggressive, they might minimize their actions to render these actions more acceptable to society. The group members help clients to learn that others might not view the world in the same manner. This is a vital part of the group process and dynamics.

If Mike "snitched" on Judy for the dirty house, he thought that Children Services would take his daughter away from him, put her up for adoption, and he would be unable to see her again. He perceived a world without his daughter and Judy as very painful. Mike's Perceived World did not match his Quality World. He thought that he could lose his daughter and her mother. Mike believed that he has always had a good, caring, and non-violent relationship with his daughter.

# Comparing Place

The comparing place is where the real world as perceived by the person and evaluated in the perceived world is compared. The differences are evaluated to determine if a total behavior action has to be taken in an attempt to bring the perceived world and the quality world into equilibrium. Our total behavior is our best attempt at the time to act upon, or deal with, the real world so we can best satisfy our needs and the pictures from our quality world that addresses those needs. We become aware that our quality world picture is not the same as the perceptions that we have of the real world, so we try to bring the two into balance. When there is little or no commonality between our perceived world and our quality world, we experience a brief involuntary total behavior that is usually painful and then go on to create a new organized behavior to correct the situation and bring the two back into balance. This total behavior will always be our best attempt at the time to try to take more effective control of the situation. We may find out shortly after making the attempt that is was not effective and, in fact, may have made the situation worse or more out of balance. This is often the case when people use violence and force to gain control of others. Some people's total behavior to being the balance the out of balance in our comparing place is quiet visible. These efforts may or may not be effective, but they all represent attempts to restore a sense of inner balance and control over the situation.

Mike was afraid to use Child Protective Services to assist in getting the home cleaned up and safe for his daughter. He thought that if CPS came to the home and saw it the way he perceived it, they would take his daughter away from Judy. He thought that they would put his daughter in a foster home, because he had the prior domestic violence conviction, and would not be judged fit to take care of his daughter. When I explained the operation of CPS to Mike, the additional information allowed him to come to a different belief and solution to his problem. He called CPS and asked them to come and make an assessment of Judy's apartment and living conditions. When the social worker perceived the apartment, the social worker asked Judy to clean it up to a point below Mike's expectations, but where it provided safety for their daughter. Judy complied and CPS was satisfied and closed the case. Mike was relieved that his child had not been taken away from Judy and satisfied by the outside evaluation of the apartment.

Mike thought that if the other man came into Judy's life he would take Mike's place in his daughter's life too. He thought that he would lose her to this man just like he lost his son from the previous relationship. Mike thought that he was between a rock and a hard place. Mike could not figure any other way to take control of the situation. His behavioral system suggested Mike had to take over and make things right. He could not think of any other things to do to take more effective control of the situation. He had to take care of things the only way his behavioral system could suggest. Mike had to step in and make things right.

## Behavioral System

Our behavioral system has the capability of storing and organizing previous behaviors. The system categorizes them as to their ability to balance the comparing place. It can also create new total behaviors to bring effective control into our lives. When our worlds are in balance and we are in effective control of our lives, we tend to pay little attention to what we are continually creating in the way of total behaviors. We are on automatic control. When we encounter a situation in which our automatic control has not balanced our worlds, we then develop more creative total behaviors. We become desperate for something more effective than what we have been using. Our creative behaviors may not seem effective to others, but they are the best that we generate at the time. Sometimes our creative behaviors seem self-destructive or painful to others, especially when force and aggression are used. Aggression has the end result of distancing others from us and not satisfying our love and belonging need. Remember, the best total behavior is one that helps to satisfy all five of the needs, not one at the cost of another.

Much of our group work is creating behaviors that will help us to gain effective control of our lives while not attempting to control others. The first of the ten axioms, "The only person whose behavior we can control is our own." is discussed many times in the group. It is one of the hardest axioms to really accept. Another element of Choice Theory that is often referred to in the group is the ultimate question—

> *If I do or say (Fill in the blank), will it bring us closer together (caring habits) or will it push us further apart (deadly habits)?*

The habits are given by Dr. Glasser in many of his books. They are:

| ■ Seven Deadly Habits | ■ Seven Caring Habits |
|---|---|
| ❑ Criticizing | ❑ Supporting |
| ❑ Blaming | ❑ Encouraging |
| ❑ Complaining | ❑ Listening |
| ❑ Nagging | ❑ Accepting |
| ❑ Threatening | ❑ Trusting |
| ❑ Punishing | ❑ Respecting |
| ❑ Rewarding to control | ❑ Negotiating differences |

Mike's prior behavior taught him that he could overpower others to get what he wanted. He had been raised in a tough neighborhood where he got his way by overpowering others. Mike had been a Marine in Viet Nam and had learned that "might makes right" so, if you wanted something, all you had to do was take it. He did not stop to think about the response that the real world might have to his total behavior. Nor, did he stop to consider his caring feelings for Judy and his daughter. Had he done so, Mike might have slowed his aggressive advance and used some of the caring habits such as listening, trusting, and respecting. Instead Mike used the deadly habits of complaining, blaming, criticizing, and threatening. He let his feelings of powerlessness dictate his total behavior.

When Mike used the CPS to evaluate Judy's apartment living conditions, he used a new set of total behaviors in his behavioral system. This is the learning that goes on while the clients are members of the group.

# Total Behavior

Total behavior consists of four inseparable components. They are *thinking, acting, feeling,* and *physiology.* Similar to the picture of the car, the front two wheels steer the car, the thinking and acting are the ones that we can consciously control. The rear wheels represent the last two—feeling and physiology—and they are created as a result of the body's reaction to the incident, what you think about it, and the actions that you take as a result from the behavioral system. Many therapists think these are the driving force behind the actions we take, but Choice Theory teaches us *we have cognitive control of the body forces and can determine our best plan of actions.* That is, we can steer the car by the front wheels and control the force on the gas peddle, but we cannot steer the car by the rear wheals.

Powerlessness is experienced by an individual when things do not go as desired. This feeling generates frustration. The aggressor becomes frustrated over current events, frustrated over surrounding conditions, frustrated over not being able to accomplish desired tasks, or frustrated with other people's actions/behaviors.

Powerlessness is the underlying feeling in the generation of anger within the physical body. All of the other feelings of anger stem from the original sense that you cannot be more powerful than some event, concept, or someone. Something or someone else appears to be controlling you or what is happening to you. The aggressor thinks that he is the victim of external control. Remember, it is not the external control that makes him angry. It is how he chooses to totally behave regarding that powerlessness that he feels that leads to his choice to anger.

Power gives a perception of being in control and it is heightened by an increased energy level. Therefore, power and anger can have the same feeling. The more successful the use of anger is to control others, the more it is used even if it is destructive to the life of the user. As a young person, anger worked to get our parents to satisfy our needs—the crying of a baby brings food, clean diapers, and gets us picked up and held, etc. If we are allowed to use anger to get our needs satisfied when we grow up, we never learn how to negotiate our needs and to solve problems for our selves. Some call this maturing, and if so, then the clients are asked to mature in the group so that they can get their needs met without the use of aggression.

Anger is often expressed as:

- Non-support, silence, sabotage,

- Tone of voice, volume of voice,

- Throwing items in the presents of spouse,

- Throwing items at spouse,

- Throwing the spouse herself,

- Hitting walls, tables and other items,

- Hitting spouse or children.

Powerlessness is a necessary feeling for the expression of anger and is always present when a person feels and expresses anger. The feeling of powerlessness has not been determined to be sufficient, in and of itself, to cause anger or a violent expression of anger. Other factors of total behavior must be present to generate the violent expression of anger. The manner in which angering is expressed is dependent upon many factors and their presence, or absence, at the moment of feeling powerless. The thought of being less than sufficient to control a situation is often present when the feeling of powerlessness occurs.

Some of these factors and their relationship to the expression of anger are well known. Others are subtle and do not always contribute to violence with anger. Alcohol is one of the most prevalent factors in the acting out of anger in a violent manner toward another person. It reduces self-control and allows a violent person to act out his anger in violent ways. There are additional preconditions that may be present which add to the expression of violent anger. These include the beliefs in a behavioral system such as:

- Violence is OK to use to get your way.

- There is a king of the castle.

- The man is the boss.

- I am right!

The behavioral system contains over-learned behaviors, i.e. behaviors that have been used successfully for many years. Over-learned behaviors are very difficult to manage. Anger is an over learned behavior. Getting angry and acting out WORKS from childhood to adult life. The success of anger/violence is learned and utilized until it becomes "second nature." People lie to themselves to justify the anger. The lies are thought to be true (by the person) and result in justification for violence. Anger wears many masks:

- The mask of stress and anxiety,
- The mask of entitlement,
- The mask of control,
- The mask of fantasy,
- The mask of shame, and
- The mask of embarrassment.

Mike described his total behavior as:

**Acting**—when operating on autopilot, Mike's behavioral system had him act out his total behavior in violence and an aggressive act.

**Physiology**—Mike was tense, agitated, and had an elevated heart rate, i.e. physiology of anger.

**Feeling**—Mike had feelings of frustration, desperation, terror, and unhappiness.

**Thinking**—Mike thought he was powerless to change things; he had terrifying thoughts of danger to his daughter and losing Judy; and he felt that he had to take things into his own hands and fix them.

Mike admitted in group, that he did not use the thinking component as frequently as he could and stated he would like to make a change in his behavioral system, i.e. think before you act. In particular think about what the reaction of the real world will be if you take a particular action. If the reaction of the real world would be contrary to the desired outcome, then try to think of a different total behavior or ask others for guidance and suggestions of others' total behaviors that he could consider.

# Real World

The existence of the real world is known, but cannot be perceived accurately. We use the real world to satisfy our basic needs, but only through our own perceptions. The real world consists of facts, concepts, and items. We can assess the effect of the facts on our lives, but the concepts are cognitive in nature and the understanding of them is modified by our perceptions. Similarly, the essentials of the real world can only be perceived through our senses—touch, smell, taste, sound, and sight. The actions of the real world in response to our total behavior can be evaluated and labeled.

In Mike's case, the real world reacted in a way that he thought was "harsh." The real world reacted to his total behavior by arresting him for vandalism because of the broken bedroom door, placing him in jail for 30 days, and fining him $350 plus court costs. The court also required him to perform 20 days of community service, and to attend 52 weeks of domestic violence classes of two hours each week. In addition, Judy did not want to have Mike around her or their daughter, when he was acting in a violent manner, so she obtained a restraining order against Mike. The court did give Mike monitored visitation with his daughter, but Judy could not be the monitor and she had to approve of the monitor that Mike choose.

The court wanted Mike to change to the level of a non-violent person who would not react to his frustrations with violence. The punishment that the court issued happened to include a class in Choice Theory. This allowed Mike to take a different approach in his life's decisions and attitudes. This additional information is what he used to make a self assessment of his behavioral system and consider making some changes in it.

# 7

# Group Solution

The group assists in supporting and providing the caring habits to their members. The real world's reaction to his total behavior was sufficiently drastic to teach Mike that his choice of behaviors was unacceptable. A better choice for Mike would have been one where he could maintain his freedom and still have satisfied his survival and love and belonging needs. Mike was able to evaluate his behavior and determine where he could have made better choices by discussing each of the elements of the chart. The elements of his quality world ("snitching"), the importance of his freedom need, how Child Protective Services can assist in getting his love and belonging and survivability needs met were evaluated. Mike was also able to realize how his past training and parenting established a behavioral system that did not serve him well in times of crisis. Mike learned that his total behavior could be non-productive when he did not think about the reaction that the real world might have before he became violent. The discussion in class gave Mike the information that Children Services seldom takes children from parents for a dirty home unless the parents cannot get the home cleaned up and safe for the children. Mike also learned that a change to using the seven caring habits could strengthen his relationship with Judy. The result of that change might lessen Judy's desire to be with the other men. Mike would become more attractive to Judy. This would help to satisfy his love and belonging need.

# Mike's Current Situation

Mike completed the homework assignment by answering the questions in the four areas: Wants, Behavior, Assessment, and Plan. His wants included having Judy and his daughter in his life. Mike wanted to be the only love of Judy, as well as, the only father figure for his daughter. Mike realized he would have to earn these positions and that they would not just be granted to him. Mike realized that his past behavior system had failed him in his family situation. He would have to change some of the elements in his behavior system in order to turn his relationships around and realize his wants. Mike assessed his behavior and realized that his attitude was driving Judy and his daughter away. This was contrary to his wants, so Mike decided to use the caring habits instead of the deadly habits of external control to accomplish his goals of a happy family.

Mike and Judy decided to reunite. Mike cleans the apartment to his satisfaction and is accepting of Judy's lack of a need for tidiness. Mike continued in Domestic Violence groups and shared his Choice Theory successes. Mike concluded his 52 weeks in the group, but still struggles with the use of force and anger to solve his problems. He has not acted out with violence since initially joining the group. Mike supported others in finding better choices to their situations while he was in the group. These new choices satisfy their needs and wants instead of forcing their way on others.

| CHOICE THEORY IDEAS | QUESTIONS YOU CAN ASK YOURSELF | FILL IN YOUR ANSWERS HERE, KEEPING CHOICE THEORY IN MIND |
|---|---|---|
| **BASIC NEEDS**<br>• SURVIVAL<br>• BELONGING<br>• POWER<br>• FREEDOM<br>• FUN<br>**QUALITY WORLD:**<br>SPECIFIC PICTURES OF PEOPLE, THINGS, SYSTEMS OF BELIEF LINKED TO THE NEEDS | • What do I need in this situation?<br>• What specifically do I want that I am not getting?<br>• What do I see in my real world that is not matching my quality world pictures?<br>• What is my ideal picture? | **Wants:** Mike wanted relationships with Judy and his daughter that would satisfy his need for love and belonging. Mike did not feel that he was getting his need met and was afraid that he would be put out of their lives by this other man. He saw this other man taking his place with Judy and his daughter. His ideal picture has all three of them together and happy. |
| **TOTAL BEHAVIOR**<br>ACTING \ I CAN<br>THINKING / CONTROL<br>FEELING \ INDIRECTLY CONTROLLED<br>PHYSIOLOGY / BY WHAT I CHOOSE TO DO | • Which component of my total behavior have I been focusing on to get what I want?<br>• What choices am I making to get my needs met?<br>• In my relationships with other, what am I choosing to do? Are we moving closer or further apart?<br>• Am I using any of the seven deadly habits? | **Behavior:** Mike was focusing on his feelings of separation and used acting to force his solution on everyone. Mike was choosing his old behavior patterns of external control to get his way. They were moving him away from Judy and his daughter. He was using threats to try to get his way with Judy and his daughter. |

| CHOICE THEORY IDEAS | QUESTIONS YOU CAN ASK YOURSELF | FILL IN YOUR ANSWERS HERE, KEEPING CHOICE THEORY IN MIND |
|---|---|---|
| MY ASSESSMENT OF THE CHOICES I HAVE BEEN MAKING | • Whose behavior can I control?<br>• Is my behavior working for me? If not …<br>• Is what I am doing now going to get me more or less of what I want?<br>• Am I using external control in my relationships?<br>• Am I happy or unhappy with my current relationship? | Assessment: Mike realized that his total behavior was counterproductive and that he can control only himself. He realized that his behavior was actually moving him further away from his quality world and that the use of external control was making him unhappy in his current relationship. |
| TRUSTING MY CREATIVITY, I CAN MAKE A PLAN TO BE MORE EFFECTIVE | • What can I do today that will improve my relationships?<br>• If what I am choosing to do to get what I want is not working, what else could I do that might be more effective?<br>• What is my plan?<br>• Can my plan be started today and is it dependent only on my own behavior? | Plan: Mike decided to try using the Caring habits and to stop trying to force the situation. He made a plan to use Choice Theory in his behavior and let Judy see that he had changed. He thought that this would attract her instead of forcing her to be in a relationship with him. |

Another example of how the group provides support to its members is demonstrated by the story of Paul. Paul participated in the group discussions about Choice Theory and was beginning to take responsibility for his actions and admit that he had used external force to control his girlfriend. He had been violence-free since coming to the group. He was demonstrating an understanding of and practiced positive conflict resolution skills. Paul demonstrated an understanding that the use of coercion or violent behavior to maintain dominance is unacceptable in an intimate relationship. He had not made threats to harm anyone in any manner.

## *Paul's Story*

*Our group sessions are two hours long with a 10 minute break. During one session, we were discussing an event where the police had been video taped kicking and hitting a man with little apparent reason. The community was up in arms over the situation and was waiting for the outcome of the three independent investigations that were being conducted. I had discussed the situation with some police officers and heard their perception of the situation. They also gave some suggestions of the things that could have occurred that might contribute to the credibility of the police's actions.*

*The discussion centered on the use of force and the choice of angering by the police officers. Several of the group members expressed the opinion that the police were allowed to use force and, yet, they were in the group because they used force. They did not think that it was just. We discussed the use of external control by the community and the role that they could play in changing their immediate community by teaching their families about Choice Theory and by using it themselves in their total behaviors.*

*After the break Paul came back to the group late. He explained that he had just been told that his brother had just been shot in New York and that he was in critical condition. I asked him how he was feeling and he responded that he was angry, afraid for his brother, and sad over the situation. This was his younger brother, "the baby in the family" and Paul had been careful to make sure that he attended school and stayed away from the community of gangs in his neighborhood. Paul wanted his brother to grow up "right" and make something of himself. I asked Paul about the other elements of total behavior and he responded that he was tense and anxious and wanted to "get rid of the energy that he felt inside." He thought he wanted to go back to New York and take care of matters himself. He was sitting in his chair with his head hung low and looked as though he was about to cry.*

*The other members of the group joined in the discussion by showing him compassion and caring about him and his brother. They suggested alternate actions that he could take that might bring about better results than "taking care of those who shot his brother." They suggested that he call his mother to get the latest facts about his brother's condition before making any decisions. They suggested that he use the local law enforcement to deal with the situation and that he provide them with any information that he might obtain which would help police catch the aggressors. They suggested that he pray and stated that they would pray for his brother's recovery. One man suggested that he come over to his house for the night so that he could be with someone who cared and understood what he was going through. This man had a similar experience with a good friend. The group supported Paul and by the end of the session, they had discouraged Paul from taking revenge and using violence to settle his feelings of powerlessness and anger. They encouraged him not to use external control to correct this perceived wrong.*

*As the time came for the group to end, the only comment that I could make was that I was very proud of the way they had come to Paul's aid and the use of Choice Theory to do so. These men were practicing what we had been learning in the previous sessions. Choice Theory works with aggressors of domestic violence. They can learn it and use it in their everyday lives instead of resorting to violence and external control.*

# 8

# Conclusion

We satisfy the five basic needs of *survival, love and belonging, power, freedom,* and *fun* by the ideal world. We create the ideal world in our minds by storing memories of the very pleasurable experiences we encounter and the dreams of the experiences we have. This ideal world is called the *quality world*. When we perceive that our total behavior meets our basic needs the result is happiness and mental health. When our basic needs are not met, we feel unhappiness which results in frustration, anger, and violence.

We are responsible for everything we do—no one else, just us! Reality Therapy with Choice Theory states that we choose all we do. The total behavior concept explains that we choose all behavior and that all behavior consists of four inseparable components: *acting, thinking, feeling,* and *physiology*. We can consciously choose the first two: how we act and what we think. We have indirect control over most of our feelings and some over our physiology. There is a large amount of creativity in almost every important total behavior that we choose. We choose all of our behavior and we are, therefore, responsible for all we choose.

Angering results from the perception that we are powerless over persons, places, or things and we want to control them to our satisfaction. Angering starts with the frustration from not being able to make things the way that we want them. As the frustration goes unsatisfied or denied, our anger increases. If we choose aggression as a component of our total behavior to deal with this frustration will be detrimental to our relationships and health. We tell ourselves lies to justify our aggression and to deny its effect on our lives. Angering leads to decreased problem solving, verbal and physical aggression, and often to a community reaction via the court system.

Judges use the 52-week domestic violence program in cases of anger management, when domestic partners are involved, even though there was no violence perpetrated on the partner. A man was sentenced to the group because he and his partner were caught engaging in rough sex. The neighbors and police thought that there was a fight going on in the apartment because of the noises that could be overheard. Another man proved in court that he did not touch or threaten his partner and that his partner was fabricating the incident. He was still sentenced to 52 weeks because the judge stated that when they argued verbally they must have been disturbing the peace. One of the questions that arise is, "Is this appropriate application of the 52-week program?" My answer is: Choice Theory and reality therapy are applicable to all individuals who have difficulty with angering in their relationships. Exposure to Choice Theory certainly will not hurt anyone and it is each person's choice to use the principles or not.

My primary responsibility as a facilitator of domestic violence groups is to create a satisfying relationship with my clients and from this relationship, to teach them to find increasingly healthier ways to relate to others in their lives. One of the questions that the facilitator is constantly considering is, "What is the effectiveness of the client's choices?" The client's reports of their choices in their relationships reveal the answer to this question. The facilitator is constantly teaching Choice Theory to the clients and helping them plan their future goals.

My experience as a facilitator of domestic violence batterers groups for over a decade in Los Angeles probation sanctioned programs has taught me that there are some personalities that are extremely difficult or impossible to treat with a group program, even one based on Choice Theory. They are a small proportion of the total of aggressors and they cannot be identified by the court system in advance. People who have been raised in cultures where male domination over women is the norm and who will not give up those beliefs in their quality world often learn that it is illegal to treat a woman in that fashion, but do not surrender the belief and total behavior of forcing others to do their bidding. People who are too immature to give up the belief that they can control their world with force as the world controls them with force often repeat the aggressive behavior. Additionally those with sociopathic or psychotic disorders have difficulty in understanding and accepting the tenants of Choice Theory. The seventh axiom of Choice Theory states that all we can give or get from other people is information. How we deal with that information is of our or their choice. This is true, but some clients have a difficult time adjusting to its reality.

As the client progresses through the 52 weeks, he is learning to evaluate the ultimate question before totally behaving with deadly habits.

*If I do or say (Fill in the blank), will it bring us closer together (caring habits) or will it push us further apart (deadly habits)?*

As facilitator, I can make an evaluation of the client's acceptance of the concept of Choice Theory by listening to him speak. Additionally, the client's commitment to live a life without violence as the first solution to his frustrating and angering is evaluated. We're not just talking about a difference in the language that he uses, but in the examples that he gives regarding his dealings with others. The manner in which he thinks becomes apparent and is expressed in the words and the tone of voice he uses. The client demonstrates this language when talking about his partners, both former and present. I can also make an assessment of the client's commitment to the concepts of living life with Choice Theory and without aggression. Choice Theory is a way of living, acting and being in society. It's not just a book-learned theory, but a way of life in total. Using Choice Theory eliminates the need for angering in the family. Choice Theory has proven to be an effective theory for use with persons who are aggressors within the family. It can be extrapolated to all persons who have frustrating situations in their life.

# PARTIAL ANNOTATED BIBLIOGRAPHY

Dr. Glasser created annotated bibliographies in Appendix C of *Every Student Can Succeed* (2004) and on the William Glasser Institute website, www.wglasser.com, of the following books and it is included here to assist the reader in understanding the purpose of each of the books. This is not a complete annotated bibliography of all of the books that are referenced in *Angering in the Family*, but does include some of the more often referenced books used in developing the concepts discussed in the text.

*For Parents and Teenagers, Dissolving The Barrier Between You And Your Teen.* In this book, Dr. Glasser asks parents to reject the "common sense" that tells them to "lay down the law" and ground teens, or "coerce" them into changing their behavior. Instead he offers a Choice Theory approach and suggests that the teenager's behavior is more likely to be in harmony with the parent's wishes when there are fewer efforts to exert control.

*Warning: Psychiatry Can Be Hazardous To Your Mental Health.* This is the first major book that focuses on mental health, rather than mental illness. Dr. Glasser discusses the hazards of being diagnosed as mentally ill; being treated for a non existent illness, often with harmful brain drugs, and worst of all being told there is nothing you can do for yourself. In this book you will learn that you can, in fact, do a lot for yourself.

*Counseling With Choice Theory, The New Reality Therapy*, formerly titled *Reality Therapy In Action*. This book is the expanded, clarified, updated version of Reality Therapy. Dr. Glasser invites the reader to sit with him while he counsels a variety of clients and reveals the explicit core of his counseling method, sharing his thoughts as the counseling proceeds.

*Choice Theory, A New Psychology of Personal Freedom.* This book is the basic theory for all Dr. Glasser's work. Choice Theory is a non-controlling psychology that gives us the freedom to sustain the relationships that lead to healthy, productive lives.

*Getting Together and Staying Together.* Dr. Glasser joins with his wife, Carleen, to examine the questions of why some marriages work and others fail. The Glassers advise readers on how to create loving and happy relationships by applying Choice Theory.

*The Language of Choice Theory.* This book gives special examples of how to use choice theory language in parenting, marriage, school, and work; imagined typical conversations in real-life situations comparing controlling or threatening responses with those using choice theory.

*Choice Theory in the Classroom.* This book translates choice theory into a productive, classroom model of team learning with emphasis on satisfaction and excitement.

*The Quality School, Managing Students Without Coercion.* This book develops the concept of a Quality School where there is no failure because all students are doing competent work and many are doing quality work.

*Every Student Can Succeed.* This is the most useful book for teachers. It takes teachers to a new level of excellence and demonstrates what to do and say to reach the challenging students that a teacher faces. By the end of the first year, school can be a joyful, connecting place in which all students will learn and many more will gain competence.

*Reality Therapy for the 21st Century.* This book gives immediately useable skills and techniques highlighting lead management and cross-cultural applications, and answers questions about research supporting the effectiveness of quality schools.

# REFERENCES

Abrahams, Nadine; Casey, Kathleen; and Daro, Deborah; (1989). *Teachers Confront Child Abuse: A National Survey of Teachers' Knowledge, Attitudes, and Beliefs.* Chicago: National Committee to Prevent Child Abuse, working paper no. 846, p. 10.

American Humane Association. (1994). *Child protection leader: Domestic violence and child abuse.* Englewood: American Humane Association.

Boffey, D. B. (1997). *Reinventing Yourself: A Control Theory Approach to Becoming the Person You Want To Be.* Chapel Hill: New View publications.

Glasser, M.D., William (1984). *Control\* Theory: A New Explanation of How We Control Our Lives.* New York: Harper & Row. \*[The word "Control" has been changed to "Choice in later publications."]

Glasser, M.D., William (1994). *The Control\* Theory Manager.* New York: HarperCollins Publishers Inc.

Glasser, M.D., William (1998). *Choice Theory, A New Psychology Of Personal Freedom.* New York: HarperCollins Publishers Inc.

Glasser, M.D., William (1998). *The Quality School, Managing Students Without Coercion.* New York: HarperCollins Publishers Inc.

Glasser, M.D., William; Glasser, Carleen (1999). *The Language Of Choice Theory.* New York: HarperCollins Publishers Inc.

Glasser, M.D., William (2000). *Reality Therapy In Action* [or in paperback] *Counseling with Choice Theory.* New York: HarperCollins Publishers Inc.

Glasser, M.D., William; Glasser, Carleen (2000). *Getting Together And Staying Together*. New York: HarperCollins Publishers Inc.

Glasser, M.D., William (2000). *Chart Talk*. Chatsworth, CA: The William Glasser Institute.

Glasser, M.D., William (2001). *Choice Theory in the Classroom*. New York: HarperCollins Publishers Inc.

Glasser, M.D., William (2002). *Unhappy Teenagers, A Way For Parents And Teachers To Reach Them* [or in paperback (2003)] *For Parents And Teenagers, Dissolving The Barrier Between You And Your Teen*. New York: HarperCollins Publishers Inc.

Glasser, M.D., William (2003). *Warning: Psychiatry Can Be Hazardous To Your Mental Health*. New York: HarperCollins Publishers Inc.

Glasser, M.D., William (2004). *Every Student Can Succeed*. Chatsworth, CA: The William Glasser Institute.

Greenfield, L. *Alcohol and Crime: An Analysis of National Data on the Prevalence of Alcohol Involvement in Crime*. U.S. Department of Justice, Office of Justice Programs, Bureau of Justice Statistics Report # NCJ-168632, 1998.

Kaufman-Kantor, G. and Asdigian, N. When women are under the influence: does drinking or drug abuse by women provoke beatings by men? In: Galanter, M., ed. *Recent Developments in Alcoholism, Volume 13: Alcoholism and Violence*. New York: Plenum Press, 1997a Pp.315–336.

Kaufman-Kantor, G. and Asdigian, N. Gender differences in alcohol related spousal aggression. In: Wilsnack, R and Wilsnack, S., eds. *Gender and Alcohol: Individual and Social Perspectives*. New Brunswick, NJ: Rutgers Center of Alcohol Studies, 1997b Pp.312–334.

Leonard, K. E. In: *Alcohol and Interpersonal Violence: Fostering Multidisciplinary Perspectives*. Martin, S. E. ed. National Institute on Alcohol Abuse and Alcoholism (NIAAA) Research Monograph No. 24. National Institutes of Health (NIH) publication No. 93–3496. Bethesda, MD: The Institute, 1993. Pp. 253–280.

NCCAN, (1992). *1990 Summary Data Component.* Washington, DC: Dept. of Health and Human Services, *April,* Working Paper No. 1).

Primason, Richard, (2004). *Choice Parenting. A more connecting, less controlling way to manage any child behavior problem.* New York, iUniverse, Inc.

Ranchor, R. (1995). *An evaluation of the first step PASSAGES domestic violence program.* Journal of Reality Therapy, 14(2), 29–36.

Stets, J. and Straus, M. Gender differences in reporting marital violence and its medical and psychological consequences. In: Strau, M. and Gelles, R. eds. *Physical Violence in American Families: Risk Factors and Adaptations to Violence in 8,145 Families.* New Brunswick, NJ: Transactions Publishers, 1990. Pp.151–165.

U. S. Department of Justice, *Alcohol and Crime,* April 1998.

Westat, Inc., (1988). *Study of National Incidence and Prevalence of Child Abuse and Neglect: 1988.* Washington, DC: U.S. Government Printing Office, pp. 5–24.

Wills, D. *The Criminal Justice Response: Domestic Violence.* Los Angeles, CS: Publication of the District Attorney's Office. 1995.

Wubbolding, Robert E. (2000). *Reality Therapy for the 21$^{st}$ Century.* Philadelphia, PA. Brunner-Routledge.

Yellen, Andrew G. (2004). *The Art of Perfect Parenting and Other Absurd Ideas.* Northridge, CA: Yellen & Associates

978-0-595-35509-9
0-595-35509-9

Printed in the United States
30718LVS00005B/286-384

9 780595 355099